MY ONE FRIEND
IS
DARKNESS

A Lament For Those Who Weep

John O'Brien, o.f.m.

Bro. John

Contents

Acknowledgements

I would like to thank Shaun Edwards for the support in getting this book published. He said if it helped one it would be a success. That was the clincher in deciding to get this work out. Shaun is better known as a rugby-league legend. He is now at Wasps Rugby Union Club.

Craig White of the backroom team at Wasps along with Warren Gatland and Lawrence Dallaglio, captain of Wasps and England also supported me along with Shaun.

Shaun's friends in Stoke-on-Trent, Paul Walters, David Goodwin and Stephen Taylor also helped.

I also would like to thank Fr. John Johnsone of Wigan along with Phyllis Edwards, Shaun's mother.

All these people made the book possible in the hope that it might help someone who knows loneliness, especially the loneliness that arises from any kind of abuse.

John

Dark is the world to me, for all its cities and stars. If not for my faith that God in His silence still listens to my cry, who could stand such agony?

(Rabbi Heschel)

Chapter 1

Tomorrow Is a Long Time

Sometimes words and music suddenly catch a mood and speak to our innermost being. Once, when I was in the depths of distress, I heard the haunting 'Tomorrow is a Long Time' by Bob Dylan. These lines reflected my loneliness back to me:

If today was not an endless highway;
If tonight was not a crooked trail,
If tomorrow wasn't such a long time,
Then lonesome would mean nothing to you at all,
Yes, and only if my own true love was waitin'.

('Tomorrow is a Long Time')

The dawn of a new tomorrow, when 'lonesome would mean nothing to me at all', seemed like an illusion. The only ultimate reality for me then was darkness. When the night is long and dark, 'tomorrow is' indeed 'a long time' away.

Yet my experience is not unique. It is repeated in many people all over the world, and the high suicide rates are a testimony to this. Mother Teresa of Calcutta often said that loneliness was the most virulent disease of our world. She herself experienced for years deep pangs of loneliness and doubt, sharing in a mystical way the pain of so many of our age. (See Sarenio Gaeta, *Il Segreto di Madre Teresa*, pp. 95-103).

I entered this world of loneliness when I suffered rejection and misunderstanding, which resulted in my first deep experience of depression. During this time I told my story to a priest who seemed sympathetic, but this led to an incident of sexual abuse. Afterwards, I sank further into a world of depression and loneliness. I was very broken. I do not wish to do into any further detail, but my story is not the worst. Indeed, I have come across others whose tales are infinitely more horrific than mine. However, my experience plunged me into a dark night of near despair and utter confusion about my faith. The words of Psalm 115 (an echo of Ps 79:10) troubled me:

'Why should the nations say: 'Where is their God?'

(Ps 115:2)

I asked myself: where is my God? Others who looked on wondered where, indeed, was my God. As with Job's comforters (or 'antagonists', as Joni Mitchell referred to them), others looked on and judged that I must have deserted God.

Slouching Towards Bethlehem

'Slouching Towards Bethlehem' is the title of one of Joni Mitchell's songs. It describes perfectly the way I hung on to faith and continued to pray in the darkness. Gradually, healing began. Compassionate and loving friends helped ease the pain. Entering therapy and pouring out hurt emotions and disordered thinking were important steps too. Eventually, I discovered the value of 'being with' someone in pain.

Joni Mitchell's song is, in fact, her adaptation of a WB Yeats poem. It captures the mood of when I began my journey, that place where nothing seems to fit and everything is out of synch:

Turning and turning
Within the widening gyre
The falcon cannot hear the falconer
Things fall apart
The centre cannot hold
And a blood-dimmed tide is loosed upon the world.

Nothing is sacred
The ceremony sinks
Innocence is drowned
In anarchy
The best lack conviction

Given some time to think
And the worst are full of passion
Without mercy.

In this confusing place, where the majority are full of passion and without mercy, where anarchy destroys all that is before it, many nightmares haunt the lonely ones.

In another of her songs, Joni Mitchell articulates for me one of my own nightmares, in which the feeling of loneliness involved left me feeling that I was of no worth to any human being or, indeed, to God. The song is called 'God Must be a Boogie Man':

He is three
One's in the middle unmoved
Waiting
To show what he sees
To the other two

To the one attacking - so afraid
And the one that keeps trying to love and trust
And getting himself betrayed
In the plan - oh
The divine plan
God must be a boogie man!

Which would it be
Minus one or two or three
Which one do you think he'd want the world to see?
Well, world opinion's not a lot of help
When a man's only trying to find out
How to feel about himself!
In the plan - oh
The cock-eyed plan
God must be a boogie man!

He is three.

The words captured for me my deepest fear in loneliness that I was of no value to God and I was lost in some plan of His (referred to as 'the insulting plan' by Joni Mitchell). Still I had to face my deepest fears. I clung to what Jesus told us about God, his Father. I was like the one slouching towards Bethlehem:

Hoping and hoping
As if with my weak faith
The spirit of this world

Would heal and rise
Vast are the shadows
That straddle and strafe
And struggle in the darkness
Troubling my eyes.

(Joni Mitchell)

I struggled in the darkness of loneliness amid all the irrational thoughts that lived in that place. I have pointed out that compassionate and loving friends helped me face the darkness. I also discovered that when I could share something of my story with those who came to me for support, I could help them begin their pilgrimage of healing. To this I added my prayer, my prayer in the darkness.

There is much in our treasury of Jewish and Christian witnesses that is immensely consoling and helped me to move away from the feeling that 'God is a boogie man' to the discovery of One who loves us more than we love ourselves. This is why I chose the prayers and meditations of this book, so that they would speak to those who weep and let them know they are not alone.

One of those whose writings helped me was Rabbi Abraham Joshua Heschel, whom we will meet later. He says of our quest for meaning, to be something to someone: 'The cry for meaning is a cry for ultimate relationship, ultimate belonging'. (*Man is not Alone*, p. 33) And he also notes that 'the pursuit of meaning is meaningless unless there is a meaning in pursuit of man'. (*Freedom of Insecurity*, p. 163)

Another teacher who influenced me was St Thérèse of Lisieux. She, as a young girl, felt a great interior anguish. When she was in the depths of distress she said that the statue of the Virgin appeared to smile at her, which made her feel a great inward surge of love. This, she realised, was the nature of the true God, not the 'boogie man' she was so afraid of. Years later, as she meditated on the love of God revealed in a human way in Jesus, she mediated on his words on the cross: 'I thirst' (Jn. 19:28). She wrote the following verses:

You, the great God whom all heaven adores
You live in me, my Prisoner night and day.
Constantly your sweet voice implores me.
You repeat: 'I thirst... I thirst for love!'

She showed me here that our natural place is in a loving relationship with God. We are a need of God, a need of love.

This journey from the 'boogie man' to love is accomplished through prayer. It was then that another important teacher's writings influenced me - I discovered Walter Bruggemann. In his work on the psalms, the *Prayerbook of Jesus and Mary*, he showed that the psalms follow a pattern. They begin with a place of orientation where we believe that things are ordered (e.g. Ps 1), but life and its contradictions intervene and we are left in a place of disorientation such as Joni Mitchell sang of in 'Slouching Towards Bethlehem'. The psalms of disorientation (e.g. Ps 22, 88 etc) enable us to verbalise in prayer what confusion, loneliness and pain mean for us. Finally, we come to a new peace where we rediscover God and reach a new relationship with Him. This feeling can be found in the psalms of reorientation (e.g. Ps 145-150). Bruggemann's work, *The Message of the Psalms*, (pp. 15-25), is a little book that takes us on a prayer journey (even if we are somewhat slouched) with Jesus the Christ in his Spirit, from Bethlehem to Calvary, to the resurrection and the giving of the Spirit at Pentecost, so that we can share in His new life.

Before we begin properly, there are two others whose lives and writings gave me courage to undertake this journey. Let me now introduce them, but firstly...

Towards Shaping a Vision

One of the thinkers who helped me reach out towards others was the great Jewish thinker, Martin Buber. Through reading him I learned a number of things. I realised that it is more important to relate to God than to understand and explain him: 'In the beginning was relation' (*I and Thou*, p. 32). From the gospel of John we hear 'In the beginning was the Word.' The word can only be spoken in relation. Buber once told a Christian friend, Christian Florens Rang, that Jews could understand Jesus from 'the inside'. My reading of Buber taught me this.

The greatest lesson I learned from Buber was the following story, narrated by Maurice Friedman (*Buber 1878 -1923*, pp. 188-190). One day in July 1914, Buber was deep in prayer and caught up in a mystical ecstasy when he received a visit from a young man named Mehe. Buber was friendly towards him, but so inwardly absorbed by the mystical experience he had just emerged from that he was not present in spirit. Buber was not indifferent or abstracted in the usual sense. He conversed attentively and openly with Mehe and answered the questions he asked; but he failed to guess the question that the young man did not put into words. Two months later, one of Mehe's friends came to see Buber and told him of Mehe's death at the front during World War 1 and what his meeting with Buber had meant to him. He had come to Buber, not casually, for a chat, but to ask a question which in the end he could not voice.

Buber later wrote to Maurice Friedman that Mehe died out of that kind of despair that may be defined partially as 'no longer opposing one's own death'. Buber felt that in his conversation with Mehe, he had withheld himself, had not responded as a whole person to the demands of the situation. This meeting brought about a conversion in Buber. Mehe had wondered about putting his trust in existence, but had died without this hope.

After his experience, with Mehe, Buber no longer divided his life into the 'everyday' and a 'beyond', where illumination and rapture hold sway. He reached for the present with all who came to him, wishing to enter into dialogue. He said: 'Since then I have given up the 'religious' which is nothing but the exception, extraction, exaltation, ecstasy; or it has given me up. I possess nothing but the everyday, out of which I am never taken. The mystery is no longer disclosed, it has escaped or it has made its dwelling here where everything happens as it happens. I know no fullness but each mortal hour's fullness of claim and responsibility. Though far from being equal to it, yet I know that in the claim I am claimed and may respond in responsibility, and know who speaks and demands a response.' (see Freidman, p. 190)

Buber taught me the value of being present for those who come to me. For many years I had no-one who was present for me, so I fully understand Mehe's despair and loneliness. But gradually, various people entered my life and their being present for me helped me heal. These included compassionate friends, and I believe depression and mental suffering is eased more by the love of compassionate friends than by anything else. Compassion is the face love wears. Also, after many breakdowns, I was lucky enough to find compassionate therapists who helped me face my pain.

Another man who helped me 'be with others' was Viktor Frankl, a Jewish psychiatrist. During World War 11, he had been taken prisoner and ended up in Auschwitz, where he had to come to terms with his own despair. He was very fond of quoting Nietzsche, who said that we can live with any 'how' if we have a 'why'. Frankl discovered his 'why' one day in the camp as, during one of the forced marches, his mind suddenly turned to his wife. He tells us:

> *'As we [he and another prisoner] stumbled on for miles, slipping on icy spots, supporting each other time and again, dragging one another up and onward, nothing was said, but we both knew: each of us was thinking of his wife. Occasionally I looked at the sky, where the stars were fading and the pink light of the morning was beginning to spread behind a dark bank of clouds. But my mind clung to my wife's image, imagining it with an uncanny acuteness. I heard her answering me, saw her smile, her frank and encouraging look. Real or not, her look was then more luminous than the sun which was beginning to rise.*
>
> *A thought transfixed me: for the first time in my life I saw the truth as it is set into song by so many poets, proclaimed as the final wisdom by so many thinkers. The truth - that love is the ultimate and the highest goal to which man can aspire. Then I grasped the meaning of the greatest secret that human poetry and human thought and belief have to impart: the salvation of man is through love and in love. I understood how a man who has nothing left in this world still may know bliss, be it only for a brief moment, in the contemplation of his beloved. In a position of utter desolation, when man cannot express himself in positive action, when his only achievement may consist in enduring his sufferings in the right way - an honourable way - in such a position man can, through loving contemplation of the image he carries of his beloved, achieve fulfilment. For the first time in my life I was able to understand the meaning of the words, 'The angels are lost in perpetual contemplation of an infinite glory'.'*

(*Man's Search for Meaning*, p. 36-37)

Finding a meaning sustained Frankl through his time at the death-camp. He developed this insight into his so-called 'school of logotherapy'. If we can find a meaning, we can deal with any 'how'. In his work *The Unconscious God*, Frankl argues that in us there is not only the instinctual unconscious but also a spiritual unconscious. We long for God and a relationship with him deep inside us. In this he seems to echo Augustine, who said 'our hearts are restless and they cannot rest until they rest in thee'.

The vision of these two men, Buber and Frankl, helped me see a direction I could give my work. Buber taught me the value of meeting and being with those who weep; Frankl taught me that I could be with people on their journey to God, in whom there is light and healing. We are a 'need' of God and his love gives meaning to us. I didn't feel or have to feel that I should have all the answers, but I could be with people on their journey. I had seen the value of medicine, psychotherapy and compassionate friends. Frankl taught me the value of prayer and coming to God looking for meaning and healing.

My own pain in recovery from abuse and depression is unfortunately the experience of many - the world is full of broken people. What I have come to see is that very often in the prayer of the church, those who are broken remain on the outside.

It is to that question that I now turn.

Calling Out

One of the great lacks I have seen in my lived experience of the church is the sidelining of the psalms of lament, of cursing (imprecation), and the avoidance of such books as Job and Ecclesiastes. The difficult parts of these works are kept discreetly out of view. Yet they provide a resource to articulate our feelings, and to do it within a context of prayer, acceptance and faith. We have all been in the presence of someone who has begun to speak in harsh and sometimes crude language that has embarrassed us. Even if we understand the reasons behind the use of such language, we are inclined to believe that the person who used this language should have been more restrained.

People such as the psalmists did not feel the need for restraint, causing some Christians to believe that the harsh language of certain psalms is sub-Christian or at best pre-Christian. Some Christians censor certain parts of the psalms as inappropriate to true Christian prayer. For example, not many pray the line 'Happy are they who take your little ones and dash them against the rock'. (Ps 137:9)

However, all these prayers, even with their 'odd' little lines, formed the prayer book of Jesus and Mary. They were the language and context in which they addressed God. We know from such texts as Heb 2:14-18 that Jesus experienced all the human traits we are subject to, with all their attendant temptations. Jesus recognised not only the reality of opposing forces inside of us, but also the negative feelings that come from the depth of the soul. Mark suggested this real possibility when he described Jesus' response in one incident: 'He looked around at them with anger; he was grieved at their hardness of heart.' (Mk 3:5a). The words of Psalm 5 could have formed a backdrop against which Jesus came to terms with his anger:

> *For there is no truth in their mouths;*
> *their hearts are destruction;*
> *their throats are open graves;*
> *they flatter with their tongues.*
> *Make them bear their guilt.*
> *O God;*
> *let them fall by their own counsels;*
> *because of their many*
> *transgressions cast them out,*
> *for they have rebelled against you.*
>   (Ps 5:9-10)

1 am one who has experienced abuse, opposition and negative feelings. The works I have mentioned above allow me to bring the full breadth of these experiences into the realm of God. I recognise that vengeance belongs to God (Ps 94:1) but I still have to deal with my own anger. When we bring negative experiences to God, we celebrate His sovereignty over all that threatens us. We recognise, as Jesus did, that, placed in God's hands, even these negative situations can often be turned into creative new possibilities. Jesus' anguish in Gethsemane (e.g. Mk 14:32-42) and his cry on the cross 'My God, my God why have you forsaken me?' (Mk 15:34) show how he prayed these psalms. His cry on the cross, for example, is a direct quotation of Psalm 22:1. Then the darkness of those days gives way to the dawning of Easter Day, the day of the resurrection. As we pray the psalms in this work, we find ourselves on a journey with Jesus. By expressing our negative feelings, we live in hope that we will move from our own experience of Gethsemane and Calvary to the dawn of a new Easter day.

My experience of rejections, betrayal and abuse had a shattering effect that extended over the whole area of my life. I lived in a world of fear and hurt, and found in Psalm 55:1-2 words that would help me voice my desperation:

Give ear to my prayer, O God;
do not hide yourself from my
supplication.
Attend to me, and answer me;
I am troubled in my complaint.

> (Ps.55:1-2)

Then I pour out my feelings of betrayal to God:

I am distraught by the voice of the enemy,
because of the clamour of the wicked.
For they bring trouble upon me,
and in anger cherish enmity against me.

> (Ps.55:3)

The sudden onslaught of chaos in a world that once seemed so well ordered is overwhelming. It is like a huge flood that rushed down upon me.

My heart is in anguish within me,
the terrors of death have fallen upon me.
Fear and trembling come upon me,
and horror overwhelms me.

> (Ps.55:4-5)

I often felt like a child running away from something that frightens him. I dreamed of escaping the awful reality of my situation.

And I say, 'O that I had wings like a dove!
I would fly away and be at rest;
truly, I would flee far away:
I would lodge in the
wilderness: (Selah)
I would hurry to find a shelter for myself
from the raging wind and tempest.'

> (vv. 6-8)

1 felt angry with life and everything in life. I came to distrust everybody. The words of the psalm spoke to me.

'Confuse, O Lord, confound their speech;
for I see violence and strife in the city.
Day and night they go around it on its walls,
and iniquity and trouble are within it;
ruin is in its midst;
oppression and fraud
do not depart from its market place.'

(vv. 9-11)

The real wound came from the fact that it was one I trusted who had betrayed me. Others, when I confided my plight, offered no help, only further rejection:

It is not enemies who taunt me -
I could bear that;
it is not adversaries who deal
insolently with me —
I could hide from them.
But it is you, my equal,
my companion, my familiar friend,
with whom I kept pleasant company;
we walked in the house of God
with the throng.
Let death come upon them;
let them go down alive to Sheol;
for evil is in their homes and in their hearts.

(vv. 2-15)

My pain was not a momentary reality but a continuous companion morning, noon and night. I cried out to God:

But I call upon God,
and the LORD will save me.
Evening and morning and at noon
I utter my complaint and moan,
and he will hear my voice.
He will redeem me unharmed
from the battle that I wage,
for many are arrayed against
me.

God, who is enthroned from of old,
Selah will hear, and will humble them -
because they do not change,
and do not fear God.

(vv. 6-19)

My sense of betrayal seemed to be the ultimate reality in my life. For long years there seemed to be no way out. All the lies, betrayed trust, hurt and rejections taunted me:

My companion laid hands on a friend
and violated a covenant with me,
with speech smoother than butter,
but with a heart set on war;
with words that were softer than oil,
but in fact were drawn swords.   (vv. 20-21)

From these prayers of Jesus and the community of faith, I always had a thread of hope. I often found myself reaching out in life.

Cast your burden on the LORD,
and he will sustain you;
he will never permit
the righteous to be moved.

(vv. 22)

On praying such psalms as this one, I felt all the negative feelings and words locked up inside begin to be unleashed. I also began to appreciate the pain of Jesus in Gethsemane. He entered that lonely place so that I would not be alone. Since Jesus lives now, no more to die, my pain is also his. He enables me to pray out of faith and reach out in hope in the face of despair that seems to be all-consuming.

In this work I offer my meditations, thoughts and feelings on a number of psalms and the book of Job. I hope that those who weep and struggle may somehow find they are not alone. It is not just meditations I offer; the words also constitute a prayer. I hope that those who weep with me in prayer might, through the words of the psalms, feel the healing presence of God. The psalms are poetry. The German poet Rilke said that when we read a poem carefully, we discover many more meanings than the poet originally intended. The words of the 'psalm-poems' can be applied to our individual situations. They also act as a form of sacrament. Through the words of the psalms, we enter the heart of God who is present to us through the medium of the words. I also offer the prayers for 'those who weep with those who weep' - people who live with others who are in great pain and, finding themselves powerless to help, can sometimes only weep in empathy.

For all these people, in my work I pray Psalms 88 and 6 - the psalms of lament.

Psalm 88 is particularly poignant for me because I often prayed it when the hours of loneliness were most intense. The next psalm I pray is Psalm 8, a psalm of praise. In it I open myself up to the love of life that still remained in my heart and caused me to fight on. The next chapter is on the book of Job. I see Job as an extended lament in dramatic form. People often say to me, 'I wish I had the patience of Job'. After reading Job and his rebellious words, I wonder to myself: Would you really? The final psalm I meditate on is Psalm 73, which helped me face the difficulties and confusion that lay in my heart.

The link between all the psalms is myself and the confused world I found myself in. Their words helped me face this world, articulate my pain and place my confusion in a context of prayer and acceptance. I have not yet reached the promised land of total healing. I often find myself back in the mire of depression and confusion and have to begin all over again. I share my journey with you who weep so that you know you are not alone, and also to tell you that there are many who weep and need you.

Chapter 2

My One Companion is Darkness

Prayer of One Who is Gravely Ill - Psalm 88
'THIS IS YOUR HOUR; THIS IS THE REIGN OF DARKNESS'. (Lk 22:53)

Lord my God, I call for help by day;
I cry at night before you.
Let my prayer come into your presence.
O turn your ear to my cry

For my soul is filled with evils;
My life is on the brink of the grave.
1 am reckoned as one in the tomb:
I have reached the end of my strength,

Like one alone among the dead;
Like the slain lying in their graves;
Like those you remember no more,
Cut off, as they are, from your hand.

You have laid me in the depths of the tomb,
In places that are dark, in the depths.
Your anger weighs down upon me:
I am drowned beneath your waves.

You have taken away my friends
And made me hateful in their sight.
Imprisoned, I cannot escape;
My eyes are sunken with grief.

I call to you, Lord, all the day long;
In you I stretch out my hands.
Will you work your wonders for the dead?
Will the shades stand and praise you?

Will your love be told in the grave
Or your faithfulness among the dead?
Will your wonders be known in the dark
Or your justice in the land of oblivion?

As for me, Lord, I call to you for help:
In the morning my prayer comes before you.
Lord, why do you reject me?
Why do you hide your face?

Wretched, close to death from my youth,
I have borne your trials; I am numb.
Your fury has swept down upon me;
Your terrors have utterly destroyed me.

They surround me all the day like a flood,
They assail me altogether.
Friend and neighbour you have taken away:
My one companion is darkness.

For many years I was swamped by dark depression and profound loneliness. I looked for words to express what I was feeling but I couldn't seem to find any. There was much unrelieved pain and shame in even feeling this way. I wished I could somehow share my loneliness but I felt I was in some kind of bubble - 1 couldn't reach out and nobody could reach in. I cried to God, often in tears, but there was no voice from Heaven, no parting of the waters - just nothing. What helped me face this dark hour was Psalm 88, which has been described as one that is unrelieved by a single ray of comfort or hope. Yet, many times when I was hospitalised with deep and dark depression, and longed to fade away and be no more, this psalm of unrelieved anguish was the only thing that helped me.

'Lord my God, I call for help by day;
I cry at night before you.
Let my Prayer come into your presence,
O turn your ear to my cry.'

(vv. 1-2)

The first two verses introduce the spiritual tension that underlies the whole psalm. The first verse might be more literally translated as 'O Lord, God of my salvation, by day I cry out, by night (I cry out) in your presence'. (Davidson, *Vitality,* p. 290). Reading these words I am immediately in touch with my pain. Again 1 remember many nights in hospital when dark images of abuse returned and suicidal thoughts abounded - all unrelieved by sleep. The real and raw words of the psalm were (and often still are) the only reality I could see.

The words 'I cry out' are a translation of a Hebrew verb which often indicates a cry of anguish or distress (Ps 107:6, 28). The anguished cry is to the 'God of my salvation'. These words are addressed to a God who cares, who delivers, who helps. They recall to my mind the days when the peace of a church would call out to me - when I would visit quietly and feel peace and joy. They were also the days when I could dream God's dream of a better world. But rejection and abuse turned my dreams into nightmares - here the tension of the psalmist became my tension. I use the word 'became' in the past tense, yet it would be more honest of me to say it 'becomes'; for the nightmare of rejection, abuse and the silence of those who could have helped is a reality I experience still. My dark night is still being lived, though thanks to compassionate friends, I continue to hope and carry on. The prayers (Ps 88 and others) provide no answers; they only lead to further questioning, deeper loneliness and more and more doubts. They show me that I am a welter of contradictory and confused emotions. When I face these moments, it is to Psalm 88 that I return. Now when I pray it, I do not pray it only for myself but also for those I have not met, who feel swamped by the same darkness as I do. I pray it to help us express these feelings, doubts and fears in faith. At many points in my life, I have met people who have told me that these feelings are against faith. 1 took their message on board, and the unrelieved, unacknowledged feelings dogged me. Psalm 88 released me from this way of thinking. Harry Williams once said: 'faith consists in the acceptance of doubt, not as we generally think, in its repression'. In the context of Psalm 88, this acceptance means moving all the pain and hurt, the bitterness and unanswered questions, to God, who for now remains silent. This experience mirrors the dark nights of the profoundly lonely who reach out in the darkness. It was also the prayer of Jesus who, during his life, 'offered up prayer and entreaty, aloud and with silent tears'. (Heb 5:7)

For my soul is filled with evils:
my life is on the brink of the grave.
I am reckoned as one in the tomb:
I have reached the end of my strength,

Like one alone among the dead;
like the slain lying in their graves;
like those you remember no more,
cut off, as they are, from your hand.
You have laid me in the depths of the tomb,
in places that are dark, in the depths.
Your anger weights down upon me
I am drowned beneath your waves.
You have taken away my friends
and made me hateful in their sight.
Imprisoned, I cannot escape;
my eyes are sunken with grief.
I call to you, Lord, all the day long;
to you I stretch out my hands.

(vv. 3-9)

The complaint in verses 3-9 lays bare the crisis in the psalmist's life - and also the pain that has characterised much of my life. His complaints are mine too, and those of everyone for whom I pray these words. The words describe a bucketful of disasters that have taken the psalmist to death's door, to 'Sheol'. (In the Hebrew Bible, 'Sheol' refers to the nether-world where there is only a form of half-life.) Belief in the resurrection and life after death has not as yet become part of the psalmist's faith. He has been overcome by disaster and faced extinction.

This is the very point referred to in the various Psalms. The language used here is synonymous with the language of suffering from critical illness or facing a life- threatening situation. The psalmist feels helpless. The words of verse 5: 'like one alone among the dead', point to a man once full of vitality who now lives in utter weakness. I relate very much to these words. After the incident of abuse, mental pain soon translated itself into physical pain. I was crippled mentally and physically. I cried aloud to God, but no-one appeared to be listening. The chilling associations of death are spelled out in verses 10-12, but are also anticipated in the second half of verse 5, where the dead are described as 'those you remember no more ... cut off, as they are, from your hand'. It seems as if God is powerless to help. For many years I prayed in this darkness in the fear that my words fell on an empty darkness. Those who suffer from profound loneliness know this place only too well.

The psalmist attributes no blame for his condition to other people. He holds only one person responsible for what has happened - God, to whom he prays. 'You have laid one in the depths ... your anger weighs down on me. I am drowned beneath your woes.' In this dark and bottomless pit, he now feels himself overwhelmed. This in some ways is a difficult part of the Psalm for me. For years I felt so bad that I blamed no-one but myself. I internalised all the anger, the blame my abuser dumped on me. This led to deep depression. All I wanted was to fade away and be no more. It is this form of anguish that manifests itself as anorexia in many people. All the time this was going on inside me, I began to reject people - I wanted no-one to come near. Yet there were people who never ceased to love me. For a time I would wonder about these people. Did they not see how ugly and worthless I was? However, their love overcame even this barrier. In the light of this love, I could begin to see that so much resentment was inside of me. I was angry with my abuser, but even more angry with those who promised me help to overcome the darkness and begin life. None of this was ever done. I was left alone and fell into deeper darkness.

I was afraid to say to God that these people acted in His name and He was silent. There was a hidden resentment in me against God too. No wonder Nietzsche could speak of Christianity as a religion of resentment. The words of Psalm 88 allowed me to pour out how I felt - it put words to my confused, contradictory world.

The social ties that might have sustained the psalmist have all dissolved. He complains of becoming an object of derision, shunned by former friends (v. 8) - a very lonely cross to bear. This illustrates issues which Job complains about bitterly (Job 19:9-15) as he faces his fear in agonising loneliness.

This too was my experience before the love of compassionate friends began to shine through. Initially, however, as I drifted further into mental, emotional and physical illness, friends began to drift. One even suggested that all this had come about because I didn't pray. Job's comforters ride again. I felt like the psalmist imprisoned in an impossible situation, from which there was no escape. All life was ebbing away (vv. 8-9), yet he continued to pray. I made his words my own, but those around me felt I wasn't praying. Within myself I continued to pray but felt that my words disappeared into silence. Terry Waite describes a similar experience during his years of captivity: 'A battle rages within me and affects every part of me - mind, body and soul. It's the classic conflict between light and darkness, life and death. I continue to pray each day, but I know I am not going to be given a palliative. This battle, which threatens me with total physical and psychological collapse, has to be fought by me as I am.' (*Taken on Trust*, p. 379)

Often my prayer just showed even deeper darkness from which I could not emerge. This leads to vv. 10-12.

> *Will you work your wonders for the dead?*
> *Will the shades stand and praise you?*
> *Will your love be told in the grave*
> *or your faithfulness among the dead?*
> *Will your wonders be known in the dark*
> *or your justice in the land of oblivion?*

There is no palliative for the psalmist. His prayers only lead to further questions, rhetorical questions that all entreat the answer: no! This is one of the most negative pictures of what the psalmist expects to find on the other side of death in the whole of the Hebrew Bible (cf. Is 38:17-18, Job 10:21-22). All that is central to a rich, fulfilling, God-centred life is absent. There are no 'wonders' (vv. 10,12 also Ps 77:11), no 'praise of God' (v. 10), nothing of God's 'loving care' or 'faithfulness' (v. 11, see Ps 89:11). There is no 'saving help'. This is the land that is called 'Abbadon' in Hebrew. It is the very land of oblivion, related to the Hebrew root meaning 'to finish, destroy'. It underlines the fact that Sheol is the place in which all that is meaningful in life has come to an end. When I read these lines, at first I did not relate to them as a description of a world to come. I felt as if I was already part of Sheol - no wonders, no life, no joy. All was destroyed. Death would bring no relief or release the emptiness of this world would continue. Yet there was always a spark that would not give in. There was a part of me that rebelled against this kind of deep shadow. My prayer was a complaint against this place, and I kept a faint hope locked away in my heart that my prayer was not in vain.

Ann Weems is an American woman whose son was murdered. She entered a phase of deep grief and depression. She composed her own psalms of lament to pour out her grief to God. Her words help me reach out: in one of her psalms we hear her say:

O God, find me!
I am lost
in the valley of grief,
and I cannot see my way out.

My friends leave baskets of balm
at my feet,
but I cannot bend to touch
the healing
to my heart.
They call me to leave
this valley,
but I cannot follow
the faint sound
of their voices.
They sing their songs
of love,
but the words fade
and vanish in the wind.
They knock,
but I cannot find the door.
They shout to me,
but I cannot find the voice
to answer.
O God, find me!
Come into this valley
and find me!
Bring me out of this land of weeping.
(Ann Weems, *Psalms of Lament*, p. 9)

The psalmist is filled with a sense of shuddering dread as she contemplates a future that is no future, but she still reaches out to God. The battle rages within but both she and the psalmist of Psalm 88 give me courage to remain in the battle - we continue to cry out for help. This leads me to the last part of Psalm 88:

As for me, Lord, I call to you for help:
in the morning my prayer comes before you.

Lord, why do you reject me?
Why do you hide your face?

Wretched, close to death from my youth,
I have borne your trials; I am numb.
Your fury has swept down upon me;
Your terrors have utterly destroyed me.

they surround me all the day like a flood,
they assail me all together.
Friend and neighbour you have taken away:
my one companion is darkness

(vv. 13-18)

The word translated as 'call to you for help' is a different word from that in verse 1 and denotes an urgent cry for help in a tense situation. Here it is a cry offered in the morning - the time of a new beginning when God is expected to demonstrate anew his love for his people - but the cry remains unanswered. His prayer is very apt for those who suffer from depression. Morning time for many of us can be hell. After the release of sleep (when it finally comes), the depressed person is once again in the depths of despair, full of dark thoughts and incredible anxiety. One has to face the day afresh with every likelihood that the darkness inside will not disappear. On bad days every person encountered seems to offer an opportunity for new betrayal. The darkness of this verse really hit home.

Using the language of lament, the psalmist asks God why he continues to reject him and gives no attention to him in his hour of need. He describes himself as 'numb' (v. 5). He feels close to death, battered by God's trials, his anger and assaults (v. 16). This is language that Job was only too familiar with in the meaningless tragedies that hit his life (e.g. Job 6:4, 9:34, 13:21). These verses perfectly express what the struggling, depressed and abused person feels. I can make them my own. Job's many incidents of rejection were hard to take. Rejecting a human being is the same as killing his or her spirit. It leaves one in a vulnerable situation, which abusive people exploit. My story is all too common - I have met many vulnerable young men and women who have been broken by abuse.

26

There are many times when I and they can only cry out 'wretchful, close to death, from my youth I have borne your trials; I am numb'.

The soul-destroying experience of loneliness and isolation comes to a crescendo at the end of the Psalm. All the pain surrounds him and beats in upon him. He now has no friends or neighbours - a theme he already introduced in v.8. The Grail version for the psalm ends with the line 'my one companion is darkness'. Robert Davidson suggests that this line may be translated in a different way (*Vitality*, p. 292.). He suggests 'companion' could be taken together with 'friends' and 'neighbours', leaving 'darkness' as the psalmist's final explanation, a protest or a sigh that sums up his whole experience in one word - 'darkness'. This is a stark ending to the psalm.

I have met many people who can't bear to think that anyone could pray in such a way. They have a spirituality that seeks to say things are not so bad, 'the Lord is there, you shouldn't feel that way'. I remember once when I worked in a hospital as a Chaplain, I was at a man's deathbed. As I sat there with his family in sadness, a nun suddenly burst into the room and demanded that we be joyful, and that I say something inspiring. She made no inroads, and soon departed the scene looking at me as if I were a pig who had drifted into a feast of the Jewish Maccabees. Her intervention was totally inappropriate, and the family were devastated and profoundly hurt. The place they were at was not honoured. I suspect that at the heart of all pseudo-spirituality lies a great terror of ever having to face moments when all is in darkness and our God seems far away. The psalmist within Psalm 88 faces the reality of his situation. He writes as one who sees no light at the end of the tunnel. There are many of us who, because of one tragedy or another, find ourselves at times in this dark tunnel - it's a time when we struggle with questions and no answers seem to be forthcoming. Robert Davidson recalls how he asked a mother whose child had been shot dead in Dunblane how she coped. She replied: 'I am not coping: I never shall.' She echoes the experience of Anne Weems, whom we met earlier. I can relate to this, as abuse and rejection can lead many of us to the same place - 'I am not coping'. This is where Ps. 88 ends. Yet, for all its distress, it is still a prayer and the psalmist has a spark of hope in his heart that his prayer might be heard. His prayer has become my own when the darkness overpowers me. Accepting Robert Davidson's alternative ending, all I can do is lay before God my pain, summed up in the one word: 'Darkness'.

Chapter 3

Wasting with Grief

Psalm 6
To THE LEADER: WITH STRINGED INSTRUMENTS: ACCORDING TO THE
SHEMINITH. A PSALM OF DAVID.

O Lord, do not rebuke me in your anger,
or discipline me in your wrath.

Be gracious to me, O Lord, for I am languishing;
O Lord, heal me, for my
bones are shaking with terror.

My soul also is struck with terror,
while you, O lord - how long?

Turn, O Lord, save my life;
deliver me for the sake of your steadfast love.

For in death there is no remembrance of you;
in Sheol who can give you praise?

I am weary with my moaning;
every night I flood my bed with tears;
I drench my couch with my weeping.

My eyes waste away because of grief;
they grow weak because of all my foes.

Depart from me, all you workers of evil,
for the Lord has heard the sound of my weeping

The Lord has heard my supplication;
the Lord accepts my prayer.

All my enemies shall be ashamed and struck with terror;
they shall turn back, and in a moment be put to shame.

For this meditation I come to Psalm 6 which I see as a cry for healing. The language of verses 2-3 and 6-8 is stark and points to one who is severely depressed. The last words of verse 7 speak of 'all my foes', which leads to references to 'works of evil' (v. 8) and 'enemies' (v. 10). Attacks by people are the source of his illness. Those who have been broken by abuse and rejection can relate to these words and make them their own. The terror and hurt visited on the psalmist have weakened him both physically and psychologically. We are complex organisms - a body, mind, spirit - and if the spirit is crushed there are repercussions in the body and mind. The psalmist shows all the signs of clinical depression.

Sometimes, in the depression that follows the trauma of abuse and rejection, even those close to us, such as friends, can be viewed with suspicion, as enemies. I have often been very afraid of people, even people who tried to love me, seeing them as sources of future betrayal. I have found that living with rejection means I can reject others in turn. Praying Psalm 6 helps me to face these realities and reach out, in the hope that I will not remain in that place.

The psalm itself involves a spiritual pilgrimage as the psalmist moves from a negative plea to God ('do not rebuke me, v. 1) through a positive plea ('saved my life'), verse 4 to the assurance that his plea has been heard and answered, 'The Lord has heard' (v. 9). It's a difficult journey and the final part is perhaps a point I have not fully reached. Believing that my voice is heard involves a leap of faith. It also involves an act of faith to believe that my prayer for those in the same boat receives an answer in the silence of God.

To the leader: with stringed instruments:
according to The Sheminith.
A Psalm of David.
O LORD, do not rebuke me in your anger,
or discipline me in your wrath.
Be gracious to me, O LORD, for I am languishing;
O LORD, heal me, for my bones are shaking with terror.
My soul also is struck with terror,
While you, O LORD - how long?

Here the psalmist is convinced that the origin of his plight is in the 'anger' and 'wrath' of the Lord (v. 1). In the Hebrew Bible many authors had no hesitation in attributing a wide range of human emotions to God -

this comes from the belief that God is a personal God. There are constraints to such anthropomorphic language: 'for I am God and not man, the Holy One in your midst' (Hos. 11:9). When we speak of God we have to realise that he is above and beyond our human language of Him (or Her!). However, since we are made in the image and likeness of God, there might be something in God that corresponds in some way to our emotions. Rabbi Abraham Heschel spoke about the 'wrath of God' in his book *The Prophets*. He tells us that the wrath of God is directed against injustice, intolerance and any abuse of the person. He tells us that our language of God is not crude anthropomorphism but a profound understatement of God's care and feeling for his people. I know from my own experience that my own anger has often been irrational and unjustified. I can transfer my own view of this anger onto God and imagine He can be the same. I have come to realise, with the help of such people as Rabbi Heschel, that this is not so with God. His anger is a reflection of his care for the world of his creation, of his response to the hurt and rejection that is brought so often into people's lives by our failure to live his life of love (cf. Rom 1:18-22). The purpose of his anger is to call human beings back to who they are and to teach us how much God values each individual person. Abuse, rejection and pain are abhorrent to God, yet, sadly, many people pay little attention to these truths.

A further comment is appropriate about the anger of God. I have met many people who have endured grave suffering in their lives. These people are often very good people who have sought to put God's ways into practice as best they could. Yet they have often found that sadness and tragedy came into their lives. It does not escape their notice that there are many who do not take God's values seriously, yet who are evidently well rewarded. The people who suffer tragedy see themselves as somehow cursed, as if they have committed a sin against the Holy Spirit (cf. Mk 3:29). When I hear those words, I remember how I felt. I believed God had deserted me and my cry was 'My God, my God, why have you forsaken me?' (Ps 22:1). It was reading the book of Job that comforted me. I never found that Job was patient in any popular sense of the term - except in the prose sections in the first two chapters. Job is the innocent sufferer who cries to God and fires the question to Him as to why the good suffer, and why so much suffering comes to the innocent. He complains:

God had left me at the mercy of malefactors
and cast me into the clutches of wicked men

I was at ease, but he set upon me and mauled me,
seized me by the neck and worried me.
He set me up as his target;
his arrows rained upon me from every side;
pitiless, he cut deep into my vitals,
he spilt my gall on the ground.
He made breach after breach in my defence;
he fell upon me like a fighting man

(16:11-14; cf.6.4)

Although it seems to Job that God flaunts justice indiscriminately (Ch. 9), Job insists in appealing to this alien God:

I am sickened of life;
I will give free reign to my griefs,
I will speak out in bitterness of soul.
I will say to God, 'Do not condemn me,
but tell me the ground of thy complaint against me

(10.1-2)

It is in the spirit of Job that I pray Psalm 6, still reaching out in the face of all that seems to contradict that life is good. It is hoping against all hope and daring to seek healing. Job is much underutilised in pastoral practice, but the people I have introduced him to find consolation there and the courage to live in the face of all that is evil. It's the same journey I made myself. Job challenges the world view of the psalmist who wrote Psalm 6 and dares to assert that the innocent and good do suffer. His own suffering is not due to some unknown sin. Yet, with the psalmist, he reflects that God will be gracious to him (Ps 6:2) and heal him of his agony.

In Psalm 6, the psalmist then goes on to describe his condition. He is 'languishing', his vitality is draining away. The same verse is used elsewhere in the Psalms and in Job, about the wicked being doomed to wither away like grass burnt in the merciless heat of the sun.(Ps 37:2, Job 18:16, 24:24) In Psalm 90:6, it is used to depict human life in its brevity and mortality. The psalmist's whole being is undermined, in the grip of terror. The repetition of the Hebrew verb, translated as 'shaking with terror' (v. 2) and 'struck with terror' (v. 3) indicates the extremity of his condition. He calls out 'How long?' These words are very real for people who suffered abuse as children, who lived in terror, shame and hurt, wondering if it would ever end. As adults these people are often fearful. One woman, Lisa (not her real name), was abused when she went to a minister of her church with an emotional problem. The hurt of what happened to her ate into her spirit until one day, in a fit of deep sadness, she took her life. She was languishing like the psalmist but could no longer live with the question 'how long?'

For many years I felt as Lisa felt, that same dread, terror and languishing. I made the words of the psalm my own and today I pray them for myself and all who experience the same loneliness, in the hope that somehow the words might reach them and their pain will be eased.

Turn, O LORD, save my life;
deliver me for the sake of your steadfast love.
For in death there is no remembrance of you:
in Sheol who can give you praise?

(v. 4-5)

The basis of the psalmist's plea has been his weakness, his fear and dread, his sense of loneliness and depression. His trust is in God's nature as 'steadfast love'. The Hebrew word for God's steadfast love is his *hesed*. Many of us have been terrified at one stage or another of measuring God's love by our own failing efforts. The prophet Hosea confirms that the people's *hesed* is like a morning cloud, like the dew that disperses early (Hos. 6:4). This is not so with the Lord's *hesed*. It remains constant in the midst of all human frailty. Ps 136 celebrates God's *hesed* in creation vv.1-9), throughout Israel's history (vv.10 - 22) and in present history (vv. 23-25). In the first letter of John in the New Testament, he alludes to the scene there by reminding us: 'In this is love, not that we loved God first, but that he loved us and sent his Son'. (1 Jn. 4:10). These words are fine but people who have been abused or rejected in any way are very afraid that the words are not true for them. In the case of those who have been abused by members of the clergy, the very ones who preach on these themes, the idea of love and the love of God have been poisoned.

Paul Tillich defines faith as the courage to accept acceptance. (*The Courage To Be* p.10). His words are well chosen. In the years when I suffered I saw no sign of God anywhere. Non-acceptance in the form of violent rejection was my lot. The idea of being accepted seemed like a forlorn hope. When I was very ill, two friends prayed for me. They had received an intuition in prayer that I was gravely ill and close to despair. They prayed and somehow the love they had in their prayers began to change me. They got in touch with me and showed their concern and love. It was the first break in the darkness after many years. I appreciated why Paul Tillich spoke of the word 'courage'. In the face of the violence and rejection, I had to affirm that there was still a love which non-acceptance had clouded from my vision.

The second phase came in a strange manner. A friend of mine who had shown me much kindness suddenly revealed a depressed side of herself. She became anorexic and withdrawn and began to shut people out of her life. One day I gathered up the courage to ask her what was wrong. She began to tell her story, very slowly, as if she was not altogether sure she could trust anybody. I had just to stay and be quiet. It turned out she had been the victim of a priest who had tried to take advantage of her, which had devastated her. I shared something of my story and gradually, in the face of my acceptance of her, she began to come to herself again. I was still very ill at the time and I had to dig deep into my reserves to offer help.

The story doesn't end there. I was on the verge of leaving the ministry when my friend told me that she prayed about both of us. She felt both of us had different paths to walk and that I should go back and somehow try to help those like her who felt broken. I was pretty broken myself. I had reported my experience of abuse to the authorities, yet nothing was done. I felt as if I had nothing to offer and wondered about the sanity of my friend's prayer. However, I came back again and resolved to see what would happen. This work, and the prayer I offer for those who suffer, perhaps contains something of the insight my friend had. There are many who feel they are alone and of no account - these words attempt to share the burden of such people and to let them see they are not alone. It is a cry to God to deliver us for the sake of his steadfast love.

There is another reason for the psalmist's plea. If death is to be his lot, then this means the end of any meaningful relationship with God. To die means to go down to *Sheol*, the Hebrew word for the abode of the dead, as we have seen. In Job 10:21 it is described as 'the Land of gloom and darkness, the land of gloom and chaos, where light is like darkness'. It is a place where faith and life no longer have any meaning (Job 17:15-16). It is an insatiable monster (Is 5:16), a bottomless pit (Ez. 32:18-21, Ps 16:10) - these are some of the grim pictures of what the writers imagined *Sheol* to be. Qoheleth protests that 'a living dog is better than a dead lion. The living know they will die, but the dead know nothing ... . Their love and their envy has already perished; never again will they have any share in all that happens under the sun.' (Eccl:9:4-6). This is the way the psalmist saw

Sheol, as we saw with Ps 88. Here he denies that there is any access to God's steadfast love or faithfulness. There are hints of another attitude in some psalms (see Ps 49, 73, and B9). However, the majority of the psalms are haunted by the shadow of death.

The view of *Sheol* given above is for me a reflection of the nightmare many people undergo even now and the fear of *Sheol* expresses the fear of many in the face of death. Job's description of *Sheol* as doom and darkness, gloom and chaos where light is darkness (Job 10:21) is a perfect description for me of what it is to severely depressed here and now. Sadness, hurt, loneliness and confusion are what it means to be in mental anguish. Abuse and rejection precipitate these feelings. REM's song 'Everybody Hurts' tells us that suffering is not just the lot of those who suffer abuse and rejection. It means in practice that, with so much pain about, many find it hard to give themselves to others and be there for them. Abuse and violent rejection do lead to a mental anguish that is many times greater than that depicted in REM's song. We live in a lonely world where some take their lives and many live in quiet desperation. The psalmist's reflection on *Sheol* reflects a world that for many is already present.

As I fight mental anguish and try to cope with my own pain, I find the mornings are the time when I am at my weakest. There appears to be no relief at this hour - it is a time of loneliness, anguish and despair. I have to pray these words and pray that I be able to say 'yes' to life and face a new beginning. It is almost impossible to communicate the anxiety and anguish of these waking moments. The best description of loneliness for me comes from the poet Philip Larkin, a professed atheist who used to visit churches to pray quietly. He would say that depression was for him what daffodils were for Wordsworth. Like those who live in darkness, he hoped to reach out and find something. He describes a church as:

A serious house on serious earth it is,
In whose blent air all our compulsions meet,
Are recognised, and robed as destinies.
And that much never can be obsolete,
Since someone will forever be surprising
A hunger in himself to be more serious,
And gravitating with it to this ground,
Which, he once heard, was proper to grow wise in,
If only that so many dead lie round.

(Church Going)

In his hymn to the dawn, 'Aubade', Larkin describes the loneliness of the early morning, when many of us are at our lowest:

I work all day, and get half-drunk at night.
Waking at four to soundless dark, I stare.
In time the curtain-edges will grow light.
Till then I see what's really always there:
Unresting death, a whole day nearer now,
Making all thought impossible but how
And where and when I shall myself die.
Arid interrogation: yet the dread
Of dying, and being dead,
Flashes afresh to hold and horrify.

Waking to 'soundless dark', he sees the first signs of the encroaching dawn and all he can see is unresting death. Like the psalmist, Larkin is in a lonely place wrestling with anguish. All that is or seems to be real for him is his loneliness and the onrush of final death. He goes on to describe his fear of death:

This is a special way of being afraid
No trick dispels. Religion used to try,
That vast moth-eaten musical brocade
Created to pretend we never die,
And specious stuff that says no rational being
can fear a thing it will not feel, not seeing
That this is what we fear - no sight, no sound,
No touch or taste or smell, nothing to think with,
Nothing to love or link with,
The anaesthetic from which none come round.

This fear of death resides in all of us in one form or another. This passage corresponds roughly with the psalmist's fear of *Sheol*. Now he is lonely and anxious and fears this will be the only reality he will fever know. Those who have been abused know this fear only too well. It is only when we can put words to our fears and have the courage to at least begin to accept acceptance by which we can move from this place. Being able to voice our deepest fears with one who knows where we're at is an important stage in healing. Here, the words of the psalmist, 'in *Sheol*, who can give

35

you praise?' are a cry to God to be with us in this darkness and lead us to a new day, where we do not fear the dawn.

Larkin's poem, 'Aubade', finishes with the lines:

Slowly light strengthens, and the room takes shape.
It stands plain as a wardrobe, what we know,
Have always known, known that we can't escape,
Yet can't accept.   One side will have to go.
Meanwhile telephones crouch, getting ready to ring
In locked-up offices, and all the uncaring
Intricate rented world begins to rouse.
The sky is white as clay, with no sun.
work has to be done.
Postmen like doctors go from house to house
(29 November 1977, *Times Literary Supplement*)

In the meantime, before this new day can dawn, we have to live with the reality of our pain. The mundane continues as 'postmen like doctors go from house to house'. While the sky is still white with no sun, we can raise a prayer with the psalmist and hope against hope. This was my prayer for many years before the faint chinks of sunlight began to come through.

I am weary with my moaning:
every night I flood my bed with tears;
I drench my couch with my weeping.
My eyes waste away because of grief;
they grow weak because of all my foes.
(v.6-7)

The psalmist finds no rest in sleep (vv 6-7). In graphic language he describes wearisome nights spent in 'moaning'. Floods of tears soak his bed. He can no longer see clearly. His eyes waste away (Ps 31:9) and 'grow weak'. This signals the broken state he is in. He is caught in the grief of a deep and dark depression.

These lines are indeed written for those who weep, and for those who weep with those who weep. For many years I fought back the tears. 'Big boys don't cry' rang in my ears. There was no outlet for the tears that welled up inside me. Finally, in therapy, when I began to give expression to how I felt, the dam burst and all the pain inside flooded out. For long days and nights the tears flowed. There seemed no end to the pain or the shame of crying so much. I have seen my story in the story of others. One young man I know was abused by a priest. For years he denied it had ever happened, burying his tears inside, but he eventually developed various anti-social attitudes. He drank heavily and got into many scrapes. He was prone to fits of uncontrolled anger. People all agreed what a nuisance and ill-behaved young man he was. It was only when he began to talk of his experience that the pain inside could be acknowledged and expressed. The shedding of tears was an important part of his healing. His father and mother stood by him, waiting until he could talk. They were the ones who wept for the one who could not weep.

During my own dark days when all the pain burst onto the surface, I began to question God more. Why had He deserted me? And not just me but many, many others? Those who abused and those who covered up for them and protected them were well looked after while we were in the grip of deep despair. It was true that God's love was shown by compassionate friends who shared their love, but I knew I also had to face God alone with my doubts and pain. I never felt I had lost God but I certainly did not understand where he was. I had to live in a dark faith. I prayed and gained some understanding and I did come across various writers who had struggled with the same questions.

One of these men was Rabbi Abraham Heschel, whose work, *The Prophets,* became a great source of spiritual comfort to me. In one part where he speaks of the prophet Jeremiah, he quotes the following:

My grief is beyond healing
My heart is sick within me...
For the wound of my beloved people is my heart wounded,
I mourn, and dismay has taken hold on me.
Is there no balm in Gilead? '
Is there no physician there?
Why then has the health of my beloved people
Not been restored?
O that my head were waters,
And my eyes a fountain of tears,
That I might weep day and night
For the slain of my beloved people!...

Who will have pity on you, O Jerusalem,
Or who will bemoan You?
Who will turn aside
To ask about your welfare?   (Jer. 8:18-9:1; 15:5)

This is the grief both of the prophet and God. The prophet feels sympathy for God and empathy for the people. When the catastrophe that the prophet had foretold came, and the enemy mercilessly killed men, women and children, the prophet discovered that his agony was greater than the heart could feel, and his grief was more than his soul could weep for. His pain was the very pain of God himself - the loneliness of God when his beloved were hurt. Augustine in the Christian tradition would point out that our God is closer to us than we are to ourselves. This idea of God's suffering is called pathos by Abraham Heschel. It shows that there is suffering in God but the use of the word 'pathos' points us in the direction that God's suffering is in a way proper to him. Pathos implies God's constant concern with humans - a personal love binds him to his sons and daughters. The prophet's reflection about the pathos of God brings about a communion with the consciousness of God, that is a oneness with God's concern for the plight of humanity. The prophetic understanding of God was achieved, not by analysis or induction, but by fellowship with him, by a type of 'living together'. God's compassion is a healing event. The idea of pathos allowed me to let God in and I began to know that no matter how deep the night, I was no longer alone.

Another thinker, Maurice Zundel, moved me from the Christian point of view. Jesus, the Son of God, took upon himself all our agonies. Zundel would be enraged when people spoke of God permitting evil. He said God did not ever permit evil; He suffers it. Evil kills Him; He is its first victim, (see Rouiller, *Le Scandale,* p. 233). This he sees when he contemplates God in Jesus, and his agony and death on the cross. In another place he says that for God, human beings are God to him. (*Quel Homme,* p. 109). God's compassion for us in Jesus leads us from our loneliness and teaches us compassion for one another. God is love and because He cares, He suffers in His Love. Maurice Zundel also says that there is nothing more evil than hurting a living person. It's the same as killing God and the human being at the same time (*Hymne a la Joie,* p. 142).

The view of God's involvement in our pain that I gained from Abraham Heschel and Maurice Zundel helped restore my faith in God. It opened me to the way of compassion. However, what both these thinkers said from their tradition has not been the experience of many. Those who have been abused have only received a perversion of love, while pain and grief have closed them from God and all of human life. Remembering Zundel's words, it is not only the human beings who have been abused, it is God Himself. Heschel and Zundel point out what is lacking in the experiences of many. Their words exist as a call to the church to recover their vision of God and His concern for all who suffer, in whose faces He sees the face of His Son. The Church is called to ease this pain.

Before I leave these men, it is worthwhile noting that both were in a certain sense outsiders. When Heschel escaped Europe in 1939 and came to the United States, he could not convince people of the plight of European Jews under the Nazis. He felt in his heart that defeat was the only reality in his life. He lost his family in the death i-.imps and faced a world that did not seem to care. The following story is part of an interview he gave in the Yiddish newspaper, *Day-Morning Journal* (1 June, 1963):

> *I was an immigrant, a refugee. No one listened to me. Let me mention three examples: In 1941 met with a prominent Jewish communal leader, a devoted Zionist. I told him that the Jews of Warsaw endure in the belief that American Jewry is working ceaselessly on their behalf. Were they to know of our indifference, Jews in Warsaw would perish from shock. My words fell on deaf ears. [Another incident, not quoted here, occurred in 1942]*
> *'In 1943 I attended the American Jewish Conference of all Jewish organizations, to appeal that they act to extinguish the flames that had engulfed East European Jewry. The 'Conference' had a long agenda - Eretz Yisrael, fascism, finances, etc - the last item of which was Jews under the Germans. By the time they reached this issue, almost all the representatives had left. I went away broken-hearted...'*
> *Interviewer: 'What then, in fact, did you do?'*
> *I went to Rabbi Eliezer Silver's Synagogue in Cincinnati [where Heschel resided], recited Psalms, fasted, and cried myself out. I was a stranger in this country. My word had no power. When I did speak, they shouted me down. They called me a mystic, unrealistic. I had no influence on leaders of American Jewry.'*

But Heschel refused to give in. He believed that many of the evils we inflict on each other are due to the poor image we have of ourselves, deep down. Many of us have little love for ourselves and, hurt by others, we let others down in our turn. Heschel's protest was his writing and teaching. He saw his words as seeds that might come to fruition in some people by bringing them to an awareness of their dignity. He dedicated The Prophet to the victims of the Holocaust. His insight into God's compassion and love for His people was his way of sowing the seeds in our hearts. If we realised our dignity before God and His love for us, then we would be enabled to accept ourselves and bring compassion to others, not pain. Yet Heschel often wondered in his anguish if his words would ever be listened to, or the seed take root.

Maurice Zundel was also an outsider. Yet, as a Catholic in a school that was Protestant, the welcome and respect he found there stayed with him all his life. He made a friend in the school who introduced him to the Bible and together they studied the Beatitudes. His friend also introduced him to Victor Hugo's *Les Miserables*. Maurice took to his heart the story of the Bishop, Myriel, and the escaped convict, Jean Valjean. When Valjean took some candlesticks belonging to the bishop, he was arrested by the police and brought back to the bishop. But Myriel allowed Valjean to keep the candlesticks, telling him that his house was the house of Jesus Christ and Valjean was at home there because it was his as well. The candlesticks were his. This becomes the model for priesthood for Zundel.

In later life, Maurice would rarely speak of his friend, who subsequently committed suicide. But there was no doubt that this played a large part in his spirituality. He would give of himself to wounded people to ease their pain and give them solace. One day, when he was praying before the Virgin in a local church, he experienced a deep rush of love into his heart. Mary became for him the sacrament of God's loving kindness, and this led him to explore the mysteries of God in Jesus Christ. All of these things formed Maurice Zundel but his idealism and love were to be put to the test.

When he was a young priest he was subjected to a whispering campaign which destroyed his reputation with the bishop and afterwards he was effectively isolated and under suspicion. He refused to retaliate against the man who lied about him because he refused to hurt the man who had abused him. He lived in a radical way his concern not to hurt another human being. He would rather suffer lies, rejection and slander and all that would lead to rather than hurt the man who slandered him. He did this because he wanted no-one feel as his friend who had committed suicide had. He wished rather to bring the love he had experienced to bear. It was in this loneliness and poverty that Zundel developed some of the insights we saw above. Later on in life, he was invited by Pope Paul VI to give the Papal Retreat in the Vatican. Monsignor Montini (later Paul VI) was one of the people the priest Maurice Zundel had inflamed in his days of exile.

Both Abraham Heschel and Maurice Zundel developed their lives and thoughts in deep anguish. Their words have become very important to me and allow me to see that God is there, even in the defeat of darkness. All tears are the tears of God.

> *Depart from me, all you workers of evil,*
> *for the LORD has heard the sound of my weeping.*
> *The LORD has heard my supplication;*
> *the LORD accepts my prayer.*
> *All my enemies shall be ashamed and struck with terror;*
> *they shall turn back, and in a moment be put to shame.*
>
> (v. 8-11)

In these verses the mood changes suddenly. The psalmist believes and is convinced that 'the Lord has heard' (vv. 8, 9) and 'the Lord accepts my prayer' (v. 9). What has led to this change? By bringing his suffering to God, by praying in the darkness, he is lifted out of his despondency. This is one possible interpretation. Using words to articulate pain and being able to express what is wrong are important steps on the road to healing. The value of doing these things in worship and prayer has often been underestimated. With the onset of new life, the psalmist can now tell his enemies to depart (v. 8). They no longer have the final word. The psalmist is taking charge of his life in hope.

Psalm 6 is an event where the words of the psalmist and the healing presence of God meet. He makes an act of faith and trusts that his prayer is heard. We live in a different world from the psalmist. Such a desperate plea from depression and loneliness is not normally considered a part of our individual or community prayer. Our thinking is coloured by our belief in life everlasting. The psalmist teaches us to hold on to God in the here-and-now to call out for his healing touch in this life. It is from this life that everlasting life comes.

The end of the psalm is sometimes realised in spectacular form. John Mc Carthy, who was held hostage in Lebanon, describes a scene early on in his captivity, while he was still in solitary confinement. He tells us how the bleakest despair was changed into an overwhelming sense of gladness and joy on which he was later able to draw in times of anguish:

> *'One morning these fears became unbearable. I stood in my cell sinking into despair. I felt that I was literally sinking, being sucked down into a whirlpool. I was on my knees, gasping for air, drowning in hopelessness and helplessness. I thought that I was passing out. I could only think of one thing to say -"Help me please, oh God, help me!" The next instant I was standing up, surrounded by a warm bright light. I was dancing, full of joy. In the space of a minute, despair had vanished, replaced by boundless optimism.*
>
> *'What had happened? I had never had any great faith, despite a Church of England upbringing. But I felt that I had to give thanks. But to what?'*
>
> *(Some Other Rainbow*, p. 98)

The end of Psalm 6 was the most difficult part for me in the days of my deepest loneliness. I had no living proof that the Lord had heard and accepted my prayer. All the evidence in my life pointed to the contrary. To pray this part of the psalm demanded the utmost effort - it took a leap of faith to keep saying those words. But gradually, the love of compassionate friends started me on my journey of healing, a journey I am still undertaking. There are times when I am still plunged back into the deepest darkness. Stories of abuse affect me badly and my own experience comes back in all its power. Yet the healing power of those who love helps me face this darkness and start anew. It is compassionate friends who mediate God's love. In this sense, after many years I can say that the Lord has heard my prayers and is with me. I continue to pray these words for those who suffer in loneliness and darkness, that they too may receive the healing power of love and compassion. For all these people - and perhaps you, dear reader, are among them—I made my leap of faith and beseech God to act.

Chapter 4

The Pain of Being Human

Psalm 8
To THE LEADER: ACCORDING TO THE GITTITH. A PSALM OF DAVID.

O LORD, our Sovereign,
how majestic is your name in all the earth!
You have set your glory above the heavens.
Out of the mouths of babes and infants
you have founded a bulwark
because of your foes,
to silence the enemy and the avenger.
When I look at your heavens,
the work of your fingers,
the moon and the stars that you have established;
what are human beings that you are mindful of them,
mortals that you care for them?
Yet you have made them a little lower than God,
and crowned them with glory and honour.
You have given them dominion over the works of you hands;
you have put all things under their feet,
all sheep and oxen, and also the beasts of the field,
the birds of the air, and the fish of the sea,
whatever passes along the paths of the seas.
O LORD, our Sovereign,
how majestic is your name in all the earth!

Psalm 8 is the next psalm I meditate on and pray for those who weep. It seems strange, on one hand, to choose this psalm, because it is the first psalm of praise in the Psalter. It interrupts the sequence of prayers for salvation to say something about God, to whom the prayers are addressed. The Lord is seen as the cosmic sovereign whose majesty is visible in the whole world. The psalm also discloses that those who pray and live God's dream are important for His reign. As human beings, we all have a place in God's kingdom. The difficulty in looking at this psalm becomes painfully obvious.

George Bernanos, the French writer, expresses graphically in his *Diary of a Country Priest* what I often feel. He spoke of 'that foundation block of the soul, the very last one, that secret hatred of oneself that is at the utmost depth ... probably of every life', (p. 32). He goes on to say: 'It is easier than one thinks to hate oneself; Grace is to forget oneself. But if all pride were dead within us, the grace of graces would be to love oneself humbly, like any one of the suffering members of Jesus Christ.' His words unmasked a deep weakness inside myself. I was all out of love for myself. Abuse and the years of rejection drove me deeper into this situation. I believed I was truly ugly and somehow worthy of this treatment. All anger and hate I continued to turn in on myself. Psalm 8 and the times I pray it leads me from self-hatred to a greater appreciation of life.

To help put words on how this is so, I look again to Abraham Heschel. Certain friends have often asked me why I depend so much on the words of another. The answer lies in the fact that after the abuse, I felt all I had ever learned about faith, Christianity and prayer was finished forever. I prayed that if I was to come back to spiritual health, I would need to learn from good people what faith meant. I had experience of what faith did not mean. The love of those who prayed, and lived as they prayed with me in my pain, showed me that another understanding was possible. The discovery of the writings of Abraham Joshua Heschel helped me on this journey. In being truly Jewish, he helped me explore what it means to be a Christian and dream God's dream. I made many of his insights my own and I now share them with you.

Sensitivity to God and human beings means something to those who suffer a broken heart. As Simone Weil said, the capacity for true compassion is exactly proportionate to the acceptance of our suffering. Abraham Heschel was such a lonely person. In one place he wrote:

> *I am really a person who lives in anguish. I cannot forget what I have seen and have been through. Auschwitz and Hiroshima never leave my mind. Nothing can be the same after that. After all, we are convinced that we must take history seriously and that in history signs of the future are given to us. I see signs of a deterioration that has already begun. The war in Vietnam is a sign that we don't know how to live or how to respond. God is trying us very seriously. I wonder if we will pass the test? I am not a pessimist, because I believe that God loves us. But I also believe that we should not rely on God alone; we have to respond.'*
>
> (*No Religion is an Island*, p. 3)

It was from this place of anguish that he wrote. Sometimes he felt what he said did not matter. The words of the German Poet Rilke speaks to the pain:

There is something Fatherly,
Far-away: in still nights,
as by the breath of a star,
my soul grew small and clear again.
Here in life I am alone,
and apart from me there is only one Other,
and I am afraid, because I am farther away
from him than he from me.

In loneliness and depression we can feel very far away from God and, like Rilke, feel that in all of life we are alone. Yet Heschel refused to stay in that place. He was a writer and scholar and he would use words to teach people of ultimate reality and our dignity before that reality. His words were a vehicle to lead us from the place of self-hatred to knowing who we are before God. It is a journey I am still on, not having arrived at my destination and always struggling. Abraham Heschel's words and life are for me a living embodiment of Psalm 8.

Heschel says: 'Personal needs come and go, but one anxiety remains: am I needed?' (*Who is Man?* p. 58) We are all moved by that anxiety to a greater of lesser extent. Heschel teaches us that God is in need of us and his needs are the need of love. Love reaches out and hopes to find a home in the responsive heart.

Another reason I have picked Psalm 8 comes from another idea of Heschel. He spoke of the 'Blackout of God', and the dignity of human beings before God, quoting from the Talmud and saying he would rather face a burning furnace than harm a human being. Maurice Zundel was with him in this. Heschel complained that his vision of love wasn't yet a reality because we had driven God, mystery and love from our world. Heschel said in a 1957 address, '*Sacred Images of Man*', that one might read human history as humankind drenched in blood, dominated by wars, victories or defeats, and there were, with so many dead and maimed, so many in mourning and tears. 'Ever since God expelled Adam and Eve from Paradise, the human race has attempted to build its own Paradise from which it expelled God; and the Paradise we have built has proved at times to be no more than a vast extermination camp. There is a stigma, a shame in being human. Instead of conveying a sense of God's presence and His image, humanity too often conveys a sense of arrogance and false sovereignty. Instead of being a pointer to the divine, humanity makes of itself an idol. God is imprisoned in synagogue and in church. He is reduced to a mere slogan and we no longer speak His word.' (*Insecurity of Freedom*, Abraham Heschel, p. 164-65).

In a 1970 article entitled *On Prayer*, Heschel points to the spiritual blackout, a blackout of God that dominates our age. What we experience is not only the dark night of the soul, but also the dark night of society. God is driven out of hearts and minds. 'The spiritual blackout is increasing daily, we no longer know how to resist the vulgar, how to say no in the name of a high yes. We have lost the sense of the holy. Our world is aflame with arrogant atrocities and naked violence. If not for my faith that God still listens to a cry, who could stand such agony?' (*On Prayer*, p. 11-12).

It is in the light of these beliefs that Heschel laments the failure of religion. He refers not just to the Jewish religion but to all our failures. He sees the tendency to equate religion with self-interest as one of the great failures of religion in Western society. (Karl Barth saw religion in a somewhat similar fashion in his commentary on Romans.) Heschel says:

> '*It is customary to blame secular science and anti-religious philosophy for the eclipse of religion in modern society. It would be more honest to blame religion for its own defeats. Religion declined not because it was refuted, but because it became irrelevant, dull, oppressive, insipid. When faith is completely replaced by creed, worship by discipline, love by habit; when the crisis of today is ignored because of the splendour of the past; when faith becomes an heirloom rather than a living fountain; when religion speaks only in the name of authority rather than with the voice of compassion - its message becomes meaningless.*'
>
> (*God in Search of Man*, p. 3)

All of these criticisms touch raw and sensitive nerves in many of us. The impact of the loss of the sense of God's presence has resulted in a world where other things have taken over and the needs of people have become more and more sidelined. Abuse is one of the most devastating of these manifestations. My own image of God was distorted by these people who abused and deserted me, and all that was left was loneliness and a sense of the 'Blackout of God'. Heschel shows us the eclipse of religion, pointing to the lack of authenticity and indifference that characterises much of my experience of religion, and that of others. Sexual abuse and the lack of will to deal with it are indicators for me of this lack of authenticity and indifference. There are others who have their own experiences of abuse and rejection, who can appreciate where I'm coming from. Here I am sharing my own experience and making Abraham Heschel's words my own. He dared to say what I was afraid to say and helped me see where I was at.

Heschel studied the sacred writings of his people.

'The Bible charts human beings wrestling with despair and with God. Through the words of the sacred text, God is present. The sacred text is ultimately not the human being's view of God, but of God's love and his need to love individual human beings. It shows us God's view and God's search for the human being from the perspective of the Bible. Who is humanity? A being in travail with God's dreams and designs, with God's dream of a world redeemed, of reconciliation of heaven and earth, of a humankind which is truly God's image, reflecting God's wisdom, justice, and compassion.'

(*Who is Man*, p. 119)

How do we enter the world? How do we let God in? Martin Buber, a friend and contemporary of Abraham Heschel, uses a story to point us in the direction of an answer. In the Tales of the Hasidim, he tells us a tale from Rabbi Menahem Mendl of Kotzk:

"Where is the dwelling of God?" was the question with which the Rabbi of Kotzk surprised a number of learned men who happened to be visiting him. They laughed at him, saying, "What a thing to ask! Is not the whole world full of his glory!"
Then he answered his own question: "God dwells wherever man lets him in.'"

(p. 277, vol. 2)

Devastatingly simple! And this is the journey we are undertaking with the psalms. In the psalms we have looked at, we bring to God our often troubled souls, praying that here in our loneliness and isolation, we might meet him. Abraham Heschel writes of prayer:

'Prayer is our attachment to the utmost. Without God in sight we are like the scattered rungs of a broken ladder. To pray is to become a ladder on which thoughts mount to God to join the movement toward Him which surges unnoticed throughout the entire universe. We do not step out of the world when we pray; we merely see the world in a different setting. The self is not the hub, but the spoke of the revolving wheel. In prayer we shift the centre of living from self-consciousness to self-surrender. God is the centre toward which all forces end. He is the source, and we are the flowing of His force, the ebb and flow of His tides.'

(*Man's Quest for God*, p. 7)

The basis for prayer is the conviction of our ability to accost God and to lay our hopes, sorrows and wishes before him. We can approach and draw near to God because He has first approached us and drawn near to us. This is the story of the Bible. 'Before the words of prayer come to our lips, the mind must believe in God's willingness to draw near to us and in our ability to clear a path for his approach.' (*Man's Quest for God*, p. 9-10). The psalms are the method I use in this little work to open our hearts, clearing a path to let God in. It involves facing fears, including the fear that we may not believe in God or more exactly in God's concern for us as individuals. It involves acknowledging that we are coming from a very hurt place where vision is blurred. Prayer is an invitation to God to prevail, to heal us and lead us into seeing life in the light of love. 'For to worship is to expand the presence of God in the world. God is transcendent, but our worship makes him immanent.' (*Man's Quest for God*, p. 62). This on its own requires an act of courage. To reach out on this journey means we dare to do so in the face of much hurt and sometimes near despair.

I remember once a young woman came to me. Gradually, after testing the water, she decided to share the secret that was eating her up. We are only as sick as our sickest secret. She told me how she had been sexually abused by her father and brother. I was able to be present for her, and I told her something of my story. It was a step in her healing . She moved on from there and indeed developed a very rich and full life. The irony of the situation was that she soon surpassed me in many ways of life. Daring to share pain was the key to her beginning to deal with it. It is what we dare to do in prayer.

From the biblical perspective, we stand before God yet we are not alone. When I pray these psalms, I don't pray alone. I pray them for those who are in distress and as others come to these prayers, they form an invisible communion of prayer with me. The integrity of public worship depends on the depths of the private prayer of all those gathered in community to worship.

At one point in my suffering, I was helped by Dietrich Bonhoeffer. He too was disappointed with religion as he found it. In the early 1930s he had moved from being a theologian to a man of prayer. His analysis of why he was disappointed with Christianity was simple. If in Germany the church had been faithful to its sacred legacy, then there would not have been an atmosphere of hate and suspicion that allowed Hitler to emerge. Bonhoeffer said that a church could only be a church when it was for others, not self-serving and narrow. Both Bonhoeffer and Heschel, from their different perspectives, emphasised that before we could have a vibrant community expressing itself in compassion and social justice, the individual must first be a person of prayer. Here considerations are difficult for those who weep and those who have to stand by and see their loved ones suffer. Yet only when the greater community of the church can hear the pain of those who have been hurt can the church look at itself and the failure of some of its members. It is a step towards compassion and being there for others. (Bonhoeffer)

Before we move on to consider Psalm 8 itself, a concluding word on Abraham Heschel is appropriate to illustrate the way I pray this psalm. Towards the end of his life, Heschel studied the thought and life of Reb Menahem Medl of Kotz (the Kotzer) and his work inspired by this thinking culminated in a book entitled *A Passion for Truth*. Heschel was fascinated by this character and his compassion for the founder of the Hasidic movement, the Baal Shem Tov. He compares the two in the following way:

> *The Kotzer's presence recalls the nightmare of mendacity. The presence of the Baal Shem is an assurance that falsehood dissolves into compassion through the power of love. The Baal Shem suspends sadness, the Kotzer enhances it. The Baal Shem helped me to refine my sense of immediate mystery; the Kotzer warned me of the constant peril of forfeiting authenticity. (A Passion for Truth, p. xv)*

The Kotzer and the Baal Shem show the problem of joy and anxiety for Heschel, and these two characters embody the poles around which I pray. I must face the reality of doubt, fear and betrayal but at the same time I refuse to abandon hope and let despair have the final word.

Through the adventure of prayer I hope to open myself to healing and a renewed faith in God and life.

An Examination of Psalm 8

This psalm celebrates the awesome majesty of God, and in it, human dignity finds its true meaning. Psalm 8 can be understood as a prayerful variation of the basic theme of Genesis. It is a neatly structured and balanced poem. It moves from earth to heaven (v. 1), and from the heavens back to earth (v. 4-8), from the Lord to the human race (v. 2) and from the human race back to the Lord (v. 9). It ends and begins with the confession of the sovereignty of the Lord over all life, and bowing down before God whose nature is majestic and powerful.

Psalm 8

To THE LEADER: ACCORDING TO THE GITTITH. A PSALM OF DAVID.

O LORD, Our Sovereign,
how majestic is your name in all the earth!
You have set your glory above the heavens.

Out of the mouths of babes and infants
you have founded a bulwark
because of your foes,
to silence the enemy and the avenger.

Although the meaning of these two verses is not in serious doubt, nevertheless, the translation of v. 1 and 2 pose difficulties for those who translate the text from Hebrew. The following translations emphasise these difficulties

'You have set your glory above the heavens.' (NRSV).
'Your Majesty is as high as the heavens.' (REB)
'I will adore your Majesty above.' (Dahood).

Whatever linkage or translation is adopted, the central theme of these verses is the 'glory' of God known to Israel. The word 'glory' is often used in the context of the majesty and splendour of an earthly king (e.g. Ps 21:6). Here it is used of the divine king whose glory outshines that of earthly kings. Psalm 148, another joyful psalm, parallels the thought of

Psalm 8. 'Let them Praise the name of the Lord, for his name alone is exalted; his glory is above earth and heaven'. (Ps 148:13).

A name in the Old Testament often describes a person's character and destiny (e.g. the significance of the names Isaac, Jacob and Sarah in Gen 21:3-6;25:26,32:28). This holds true in a pre-eminent way with God. (Incidentally, the translation of the name 'Baal Shem Tov' is 'master of the good-name'.) The phrase in verse 2, 'you have founded a bulwark' has often caused difficulty as well. The Hebrew word 'oz, translated as 'bulwark', does not mean stronghold or fortress. It is on occasion associated with the ark, the symbol of God's powerful, protecting presence in the midst of the people (Ps 132:8). But more commonly, it simply means strength, which goes hand in hand with God's Majesty. (Ps 29:1, 96:6) The psalmist is here drawing our attention to a strange paradox: that it is those who, humanly speaking, are regarded as weak and helpless, 'babes and infants', that God lays as the foundation of strength which can defy all his enemies. Jesus too would speak of becoming like little children to enter the Kingdom (e.g. Mk 10:15). Paul would speak of the folly of the cross (1 Cor. 1:17-18) and he would show how God acts through weakness in his own life.

> *Therefore, to me from being too elated, a thorn was given me in the flesh,*
> *a messenger of Satan to torment me, to keep me from being too elated.*
> *Three times I appealed to the Lord about this, that it would leave me,*
> *but he said to me 'My grace is sufficient for you,*
> *for power is made perfect in weakness'.*
> *So, I will boast all the more gladly of my weaknesses,*
> *so that the power of Christ may dwell in me.*
> *Therefore I am content with weaknesses,*
> *insults, hardships, persecutions, and calamities*
> *for the sake of Christ;*
> *for whenever I am weak, then I am strong.*
>
> (2 Cor. 12:7-10)

Here I celebrate the hope that in my time of suffering, God's compassion will bring me to new life.

When people speak of St Francis, they remember him for his spirit of joy. 'Intoxicated by the love and compassion of Christ, blessed Francis sometimes used to act as follows. The sweetest of spiritual melodies would often well up within him and found expression in French airs, and the murmur of God's voice, heard by him alone, would joyfully pour forth in the French tongue. Sometimes he would pick up a stick from the ground and, laying it on his left arm, he would draw another stick across it with his right hand like a bow, as though he were playing a violin or some other instrument: and he would imitate the movements of the musician and sing in French of Our Lord Jesus Christ. But all this jollity would end in tears, and his joy would melt away in compassion for the sufferings of Christ. And at such times he would break into constant sighs, and in his grief would forget whatever he was holding in his hands and be caught up in spirit into heaven.' (*Mirror of Perfection*)

This story can mask where St Francis' joy came from. He was often depressed and sometimes believed he was far from God. He suffered physically as well as mentally but in all these moments he turned to God revealed in Jesus and received new strength in the face of all his disappointments. His joy was born out of struggle and depression. When I meditate in this way, I remember many of the little things that helped me in my life. I am not suggesting that any of these took away my pain or removed the sorrow. However, these events provided balm for my troubled spirit. I think of the times a piece of music suddenly touched me and brought me out of myself. I remember one time I saw Raphael's painting of the Transfiguration and was caught up in its beauty. I remember sensitive plays, films and books. I think too of the times when my funny bone was tickled in spite of myself: such people as Kenny Everett, the Muppets or the Simpsons often made me laugh even in my sorrow. All these events showed me that there was still a longing for joy in my heart and in their own way, they helped me leave the way open to discover God and his healing. It is not the perfect joy of St Francis but it is a step on the way.

When I look at your heavens
the work of your fingers
the moon and the stars that
you have established;
what are human beings that you
are mindful of them,
mortals that you care for them?

(Ps 8: 3-4)

As children, many of us responded with a sense of wonder and awe before the world. I don't think I ever fully lost that sense of childhood. When I studied the sciences and mathematics I delighted in the harmony of the world. My experience of rejection had the effect of blinding me temporarily to this, but this blindness was never fully complete. The French have an expression which says that to believe in God, all one has to do is to look at the stars at night. Astrophysics only confirms to me the beauty and harmony of the universe. Einstein once said, 'In this materialistic world of ours, the serious scientific workers are the only profoundly religious people.' (A. Einstein, *The World As I See It*, p. 35). Wordsworth lamented the fact that so many have lost this sense of wonder:

> *The world is too much with us; late and soon,*
> *Getting and spending we lay waste our powers:*
> *Little we see in nature that is ours:*
> *We have given our hearts away, a sordid love!*
>   (see Davidson, *Vitality*, p. 38)

We gaze at the stars and we are still left with many questions about God. There might be a doubt to be faced if there is a God or not. Most people do believe that there is a God but their question, in the face of the universe, is: can he care for me as a person, a tiny speck for a short time in the vastness of the universe? The psalmist accepts the universe as the handiwork of God, and he then asks about God and human life. He is led from contemplating the universe to the question: what is our significance for God? Two words are used to describe our human life: enos ('human beings', NRSV; 'frail mortals', REB) and ben 'adam (literally, 'son of men'; 'mortals' NRSV; 'a human being', REB). Both these expressions are used to refer to our human life.

Job helps us see the pole from which some of us at times have approached these verses. Job wonders what kind of God it is possible to believe in, in a world where the traditional religious script no longer makes sense and where there seems to be no explanation of the harshness of life's experience? Job hardly seems to know. After the collapse of his world, his attitude to God is characterised by wildly fluctuating moods, with bitterness and trust, hope and despair struggling within his soul. The friends may speak of God calmly but Job's words are tempestuous and volcanic. The God he once knew as a friend he now thinks of as a capricious enemy:

God had left me at the mercy of malefactors
and cast me into the clutches of wicked men.
I was at ease but he set upon me and mauled me,
seized me by the neck and worried me.
He set me up as his target;
his arrows rained upon me from every side;
pitiless, he cut deep into my vitals,
he spilt my gall on the ground.
He made breach after breach in my defences;
he fell upon me like a fighting man.

                    (Job 16.11-14; cf.6:4)

These words are harsh but they are familiar. In my own life there was a hidden resentment against God. If he is so powerful, why didn't he protect us? Did things have to be so hard? Other people have shared with me the tales of how they were abused by a relative or priest or somebody outside the immediate family. They felt harshly towards their parents, silently blaming them for what had happened. Why hadn't they protected them? The pent-up bitterness in Job's soul makes him burst forth into a bitter parody of Psalm 8:

What is man that thou makest much of him
and turnest thy thought towards him,
only to punish him morning by morning
or to test him for every hour of the day?

                    (Job 7.17-18)

He pleads with God to stop hounding him with troubles; he contemplates the brief, troubled frailty of human life and comes close to despair (cf. Job 14 and 17). Job helped me see what resentment and pain lay inside me. He gave me a 'voice' to speak of my pain. Paradoxically, when I was able to do this the pain and resentment began to ease their grip on me and I became more open to the horizon of Psalm 8. Being able to name and confess what is going on for us when we are in pain are important steps in healing. When we can do this we begin to take back personal power for our lives.

Job, in the face of his grief and near despair, insists on appealing to God:

I am sickened of life;
I will give free reign to my griefs,
I will speak out in bitterness of soul.
I will say to God, 'Do not condemn me,
but tell me the ground of thy complaint against me'

(Job 10.1-2)

Joni Mitchell captures the mood of Job's complaints in her song 'Sire of Sorrow' (Job's sad song):

Let me speak, let me spit out my bitterness -
Born of grief and nights without sleep and festering flesh.
Do you have eyes?
Can you see like mankind sees?
Why have you soured and curdled me?
Oh you tireless watcher! What have I done to you?
That you make everything I dread and everything I fear
come true?
Once I was blessed; I was awaited like the rain,
Like eyes for the blind, like feet for the lame.
Kings heard my words, and they sought out my company.
But now the janitors of Shadowland flick their brooms at me.
Oh you tireless watcher! What have I done to you?
That you make everything I dread and everything I fear
come true?

Later, we hear Job say in the same song:

I've lost all taste for life.
I'm all complaints.
Tell me why do you starve the faithful
Why do you crucify the saints?
And you let the wicked prosper.
You let their children frisk like deer,
And my loves are dead or dying, or they don't come near.

Like the author of Job, Joni Mitchell wrestles with the mystery of suffering and pours out her lament to God. She complains of the starvation of the faithful and the torture of the saints while the wicked prosper.

This is a journey I and those who join me embark on when we pray the Psalms I have chosen for this work. We cry out our grief to God. The question 'What are human beings that you are mindful of them?' (v. 4), is best answered for me by Abraham Heschel in his work *The Prophets*, for what he says of the prophets is true of Jesus. As the author of the letter to the Hebrews reminds us:

At many moments in the past and by
many means, God spoke to our ancestors
through the prophets; but in our time, the
final days, he has spoken to us in the person of his Son,
whom he appointed heir of all
things and through whom he made the ages.

He is the reflection of God's glory and bears
the impress of God's own being sustaining
all things by his powerful command;
and now that he has purged sins away,
he has taken his seat at the right hand
of the divine Majesty on high.
So he is now as far above the angels
as the title which he has inherited is higher than their own name.

(Heb: 1 - 4)

The point I take from this is that there is a continuity between what Jesus is and teaches and the experience of the prophets. But who is the prophet?

'The prophet is a man who feels fiercely. God has thrust a burden upon his soul, and he is bowed and stunned at man s fierce greed. Frightful is the agony of man; no human voice can convey its full terror. Prophecy is the voice that God has lent to the silent agony, a voice to the plundered poor, to the profaned riches of the world. It is a form of living, a crossing point of God and man. God is raging in the prophet s words.'

(*Prophets*, p. 5)

The prophet feels strongly. His strong feelings come from his communion with the feelings of God, what Heschel calls his pathos. His reactions come about by his reflection and participation in the divine pathos. The prophets have glimpsed reality as reflected in the heart of God. They have somehow experienced the pathos of God. God is in love with His people and a personal relationship binds Him to Israel. In a sense the prophet lives the life of God. He hears God's voice and he feels God's heart. What to some might appear as exaggeration - namely the prophet's raging against the mistreatment of the widow, against the manipulation of the worker, against callousness towards the poor - is in reality a profound attempt to express God's feelings for his people and his rage at the betrayal of the poor and lonely. The voice of the prophet is a call to leave the ways of greed, callousness and cruelty behind and to contribute towards the creation of a new world. What is of interest to me for the moment is how the prophets see the plight of the suffering one.

A single act of injustice may appear to us as slight. Every day there are injustices and little or great cruelties, and I can't stop thinking that there is nothing I can do about this, so I'll just have to put up with it. Injustice to the prophets is a disaster. What is true for the prophet is true for God. The hurting of any one of God's little ones is a catastrophe for God. Jesus' agony continues in those who are abused. The prophet burns with God's rage that such evil should be visited on his little ones. What the prophets said in the past about injustice still holds true today. God's love is for his people and the idea of divine rage is to show us God's reaction to injustice. Behind the seeming austerity is a call to recover compassion and a sense of the dignity of the other. The rabbis are not guilty of exaggeration when they say:

'Whoever destroys a single soul should be considered as one who has destroyed a whole world. And whoever saves a single soul is to be considered the same as one who has saved a whole world.'
(*Prophets*, p. 14)

Abraham Heschel offers the following reflection on our story together as a community:

'Above all, the prophets remind us of the moral state of a people: few are guilty, but all are responsible. If we admit that the individual is in some measure conditioned or affected by the spirit of society, an individual's crime discloses society's corruption. In a community not indifferent to suffering, uncompromisingly impatient with cruelty

and falsehood, continually concerned for God and every man, crime
would be infrequent rather than common.'

(*Prophets*, p. 16)

This reflection is in no way alien for the Christian. Meditation on Paul's image of the body of Christ, of which we are all part (I Cor. 12-14); Jesus' reflection on the last judgement (Mt 25:31 -46); and the sermon on the Mount (Mt 5-7) remind us of our responsibility for one another.

The world envisaged by the prophets is not one familiar to us. I have found many communities indifferent to the suffering of others. Callousness, cruelty and indifference are abusive in themselves and are the seed ground for more abuse. There has been in many places no concern for God or for any child of His. If there was only one case of abuse, it would be too much, but there are more, many more. The vision of the prophets and Jesus is a call to see how much each individual is invaluable in him or herself.

Am I optimistic or in despair? In truth I don't know. When I look at the reality of my life and those who have crossed my path, sometimes I am close to despair. Yet there is much in me that will not give in. The vision of the prophets and Jesus sustains me and I can make an effort in my own small way to share their vision and live from that place. In this way I hope to find healing, bring healing to others and in a small way help the church in its time of crisis towards a revival of vision of who we are for God and God's concern for all his little ones. Martin Luther King told a friend a few days before he died that he was not optimistic but continued to hope. I think I know what he meant!

Yet you have made them a little lower than God,
and crowned them with glory and honour.
You have given them dominion over the works of your hands;
you have put all things under their feet,
all sheep and oxen, and also the beasts of the field,
the birds of the air, and the fish
whatever passes along the paths of the seas.

(Ps.8: 5-8)

Even though in the expanse of the universe and time we are only a tiny speck for a brief spell, we have been crowned with glory and honour, words associated with royalty in the Old Testament (cf. Ps.21:6, 45:4). Our status is spelled out in the words 'You have made them little less than God'. This vision of the psalmist is world-shattering for me. For years I took to heart the words and actions of those who were abusive and saw myself as worthless. When I pray Psalm 8 and these lines, God's view is put centre-stage and helps lead me from the negative feelings of depression. I pray these lines for those who are trapped in a world-view that says they are worthless.

Psalm 82 says the following:

I say, you are God's
Children of the most high, all of you.

(Ps 82:6)

This re-confirms what God says of us in Psalm 8. It helps us understand Maurice Zundel when he said that in the eyes of God we are God (Zundel, *Quel Homme*, p. 109).

In the Gospel of John this is the verse used by Jesus in his dispute with the Pharisees in 10:34:

Jesus answered:
Is it not written in your Law:
I said, you are gods?
So it uses the word 'gods'
Of those people to whom
The word of God was addressed
and scripture cannot be set aside.

(Jn. 10: 34-35)

In the Gospel of John Jesus is the Word of God made flesh (Jn.1:1-8) and the Word of God for us is Love. Jesus lived out this love in affliction and death, and in his resurrection and giving of the spirit, he extended love and forgiveness to those who had betrayed him and invited them into a communion of love with him. Jesus bears in himself the love of God for his people.

As we read in Genesis 1, what is distinctive about us in our relationship with God is followed by a statement concerning our relationship with the rest of creation. We are entrusted with 'dominion' (in verse 6) over everything on land, in the air and sea. The word 'dominion' used in verse 6 is a different word from that used in Gen 1:28 and is used to indicate any kind of mastery or rule. Not infrequently, it is used in the Psalms in reference to God's rule: 'For dominion belongs to the Lord, and he rules over the nations.' (Ps 22:28 cf. 103:19). The power given to us is delegated power. We see in verses 5-7 that there are four lines whose subject in each case is God: 'You have made them... and crowned them; you have given them... you have put all things...'

So often we grasp power for its own sake - the 'will to power'. Thérèse of Lisieux gives us an example of an alternative will - the 'will to love'. In the 'will to love', all people, things and events must be encountered, not dominated or broken. Power issues are often important in sexual abuse - it is more an issue of power than sexuality. The abuser often has a low self- image and gives him- or herself an illusion of power by sexual exploitation and violence. They are often sensitive to their own pain but insensitive to the havoc they wreak in the lives of others. This is called sociopathic behaviour. The image of Psalm 8 is far removed from this form of dominion. It does seem a reminder of where our dignity truly lies and how we are to exercise power from that place.

O LORD, our sovereign.
how majestic is your name in all the earth!

The Psalm ends where it began. These verses (1. 9) form an enclosure around the words of the psalm. In these verses the people acknowledge the awesome majesty and mystery of the God they know to be their God. That is where all biblical thought about the true understanding of life and how it began continues and ends.

This God in the vision of John is a God of love:

'Beloved; let us love one another, because love is from God; everyone who loves is born of God and knows God. Whoever does not love does not know God, for God is love. God's love was revealed among us in this way: God sent his only Son into the world so that we might love through him. In this is love, not that we loved God but that he loved us and sent his Son to be the atoning sacrifice for our sins. Beloved, since God loved us so much, we also ought to love one another. No one has ever seen God; if we love one another, God lives in us, and his love is perfected in us.

(1 Jn. 4: 7-12)

This is how God shows himself in Jesus. It is difficult for many of us to appreciate this. In the years of my deep despair I still believed in love but not for myself. Abusive situations dimmed my eyes to the light of love. Yet the vision of the cross of Jesus where he gave himself away in love always remained with me. There are those as I mentioned who showed me compassionate love. This love opened my eyes to the love of God in Jesus. All these events were important, and still are in my journey of healing. Psalm 8 keeps the dreams of a new world alive and sustains my hope. I pray it for all who feel life burdensome but still carry on because deep within them is a spark of love and hope. For a while love and hope may be denied but a psalm of praise like Psalm 8 is statement that in spite of all, we still hope and continue to love, even if this is a very hurt love.

Chapter 5

Job, The Emotional Volcano

I remember when I was young hearing much about the patience of Job. With this mind I opened my Bible and read Job for myself, but I could not find any of the patience of the kind the preacher spoke of. Instead I found a book of tragedy where Job goes through many violent emotions. He expresses all these conflicting and contradictory emotions and moods in the form of a lament to God. Job's prayers are the cry of pain. In this sense, his words are a reaction to a previous action (the loss of family, friends and health), a cry in response to hurt. The cry of pain is directed towards God (as accusation or complaint), towards others (a complaint against an enemy) and towards the self (as self-lament). All these components come together in Job to give it the form of a 'dramatised lament'. (Westermann, *Structure of Job*, 11-12).

In dealing with moodiness and conflicting, contradictory emotions, I found Job an immense help. The contradictory nature of painful, hurt emotions makes dealing with all the hurt a difficult and painful process. Job is a mirror in which I can see my own contradictions and pain, meet God in the midst of the struggle and begin a process of healing. There are many who feel like I do. As human beings, we find many ways of hurting each other and the painful state I experienced after abuse is experienced by many in their own way as they cope with their own loneliness.

Oscar Wilde, in his *Ballad of Reading Gaol*, an incredibly sad poem of a broken man, wrote the following haunting lines:

> *Yet each man kills the thing he loves,*
> *By each let this be heard,*
> *Some do it with a bitter look,*
> *Some with a flattering word,*
> *The coward does it with a kiss,*
> *The brave man with a sword!*
>
> *Some kill their love when they are young,*
> *And some when they are old;*
> *Some strangle with the hands of Lust,*
> *Some with the hands of Gold:*

The kindest use a knife, because
The dead so soon grow cold.

(*Selected Poems*, p. 108)

In the throes of hurt emotion, the verses strike a chord. Wilde shows in these words our potential to hurt one another. There is the bitter look, the cutting word. There is the kiss of Judas. The words 'strangle with the hands of lust' are words that haunt me. The killing of the person spiritually is something that passes unnoticed by a large part of society - that is why Oscar says that the kindest way to kill is with a knife, because 'the dead soon grow cold'. It is very hard to live with a deep wound in the spirit.

Walter Brueggemann is a student of the Old Testament. In his work on the Old Testament he makes several interesting points that are of help not just in theology but also in healing prayers. In his book, *Hopeful Imagination*, he says the first step for the exiled person is to accept fully the reality of one's condition. He says only embraced grief permits newness (p. 9). The words are simple to say but, in the lived experience of the broken, the words can seem to be an impossible burden. I make Brueggemann's words my own and apply them to my condition of brokenness, and in my prayer for the broken. To begin to accept my pain in all its contradictions and confusion means finally being able to articulate it. In the context of this chapter, Job helps me articulate my confusion and he does it in a prayer context. There I hope to find acceptance in my contradictions and in this way permit myself a new beginning. When I pray this chapter, I pray for those who feel something of the same that they too might find the acceptance and love so long denied.

The scene is set for the drama in the prologue in Chapter 1, in which Job is introduced as a man of blameless and upright life (1.1), a man in whom the ideal of piety and material prosperity walk hand in hand. The prologue also indicates what the ensuing tragedy is all about. Job is a man tempted - with God's permission! - to see whether he truly fears God (1.9; 2:3), to see if there is truly such a thing as a man of disinterested faith. His family are taken away from him, then he is afflicted with running sores from head to foot (2:8). His three friends, Eliphaz, Bildad and Zophar arrive and sit in silence before the plight of their old friend. Now the drama commences.

The drama begins with Job's lament, both self-directed and God directed (chapter 3), then moves to a lengthy dialogue section (chapters

4-27). Within the disputes section the friends reply individually to Job's sufferings with consolation, yet their address quickly assumes the form of altercation and disputation. This is the experience of many of us. When pain first seizes us there is initial compassion, but as things get worse, friends become scarcer and scarcer. Sympathy soon wears away as people are reminded of their own fragility and mortality. 'We all have our troubles!' is the cry of the once-sympathetic. Job responds to friends with laments against his friends and also against God, on whose behalf the friends choose to speak and judge. By condemning others they make themselves feel that somehow they are better - a not-unusual form of argument now as well as then. It reminds me of how easy it is to speak badly of God.

Bonhoeffer, when he was in prison in Tegel, remarked that it was easier to speak to non-believers of God than it was to speak to believers, who spoke so badly of God. I have heard and suffered much from those who feel they have a monopoly on God and have greater insight than others into his mystery. Interestingly, Job's friends never address God directly; they simply talk about God. They are not challenged by his word or the reality of the situation. They unquestioningly uphold traditional beliefs and practices, denying the reality of a new situation. To them Job is a rebel. Eliphaz is the first to suggest what Job's proper response should be: 'As for me, I would seek God and to God I would commit my cause'. (5:8 cf. 8:5,11:13, 22: 23, 33:26). Job is in agreement with this and he acts accordingly. He laments his plight. Eliphaz and the friends choose to speak on behalf of God without 'committing their cause to God' (5:8).

I do not intend to go through the whole of the book of Job; I will just look at 'snapshots' of Job's lament prayer and see how I can make these words my own and allow others to make them their own.

With Friends Like These...

In the argument of the friends, the righteous person must fulfil two essential conditions. First, the address to God must constitute a return to God, a turning back to God and away from a manner of conduct that has opposed God's intentions:

'If you seek God and make supplication to the Almighty': *(8:5,NRSV)*

'If you stretch out your hands to him...' (11:13)
'If you return to the almighty...' (22:23a)

Secondly, this turning back to God must be accompanied by a confession and renunciation of sin:

'If you are pure and upright surely then he will rouse himself for you.'(8:6)
'If iniquity is in your heart, put it away and do not let wickedness reside in your hearts.
' Surely then you will lift up your face without blemish.' (11:14-15)
'If you remove self-righteousness from your hearts... then you will delight yourself in the Almighty, and lift up your face to God.
You will pray to him and he will hear you...' (22:23 b, 26:27)

Joni Mitchell, in her song 'Sire of Sorrow (Job's Sad Song)', places the following words on the lips of the so-called friends whom she calls antagonists:

'Evil is sweet in your mouth.'
'What a long fall from grace.'
'Oh your guilt must weigh so greatly.'

She puts the following words on the lips of Job in response to the antagonists:

Job:	*Breathtaking ignorance adding insult to injury,*
	They are blaming and shaming.
Antagonists:	*Evil-doer*
Job:	*And shattering me*
Antagonists:	*The vain man wishes to be wise*
	A man from asses.

I have heard the echo of Job's experience in those who rejected me.
This prescribed course of action that the friends urge on Job has the weight of tradition behind it - the tradition not just of ancient Israel but also apparently of the whole Middle East (see L. Perdue, *Wisdom and Cult*, pp. 96-119, p. 172). Indeed I believe that in spite of the presence of Job's

rebellion, the insight of the friends is common currency among many Christians I have met. One woman told me of a story about an illness her father had contracted. It was a wasting illness that caused her father and the rest of the family much suffering. This lady went to speak about her father's plight to her local priest, who said he (the father) must be suffering because of some grave sin. The voice of Job's friends is not confined to the text but is all around us. When I was very ill after the abuse, it was suggested that I was ill through my own fault and really I was just a nuisance. My experience is not uncommon. The voices of the friends have a very real ring to them. Penitence, not protocol, secures God's presence according to the friends. God will hear confessions, not accusations and charges.

Job disagrees violently. First he insists resolutely on his innocence (e.g. 6:28-30,9:21, 10:7, 16:17,23:10, 12; 27:2-6). He is not guilty, hence there is no warrant for contrition or penitence on his part. He is only reiterating something that God has already confirmed (cf. 8, 2:3). From the beginning of the drama Job's blamelessness has been upheld. His experience is something many victims of abuse and rejection can relate to. Those who abuse or reject others in any way are highly manipulative. They tell or suggest to their victims that they are somehow guilty, and in their hurt state, the victims take this on board, and find themselves condemned to feelings of guilt, which exacerbate their sufferings and sense of shame.

Job provides an outlet for rebellion against this way of thinking. His very point is that the innocent do suffer, and very often the suffering of many people is totally out of proportion to any guilt they might bear. In modern terms, Auschwitz is an example of this. The sufferings of many people in our world also bear testimony to Job's rebellion. The pain of the innocent who were abused and then broke down emotionally is the example I can most relate to.

Job's friends link righteousness with prosperity and wickedness with punishment: the good are rewarded while the wicked receive their just desserts. Job is something of a modern in his analysis of what the friends say. He uses scientific observation - his own suffering is proof enough of the fallacy. Job shows that all one needs to do is to observe human experience: 'How often is the lamp of the wicked put out?' (21:17) he asks. More often than not, calamity and justice bypass the wicked altogether. They prosper in their ungodliness with such self-assurance (21:7-13) that any relationship to God based on the promise of reward for goodness is completely negated. They can and do secure prosperity on their own terms and, in the process, dismiss God without a thought:

They say to God, 'Leave us alone!
We do not desire to honour your ways.
What is the Almighty that we should serve him?
And what profit do we get if we pray to him?'

(21:14-15)

In the end they die not only rich but satisfied (21:23-26), leaving the question of justice for others to argue over. This is the way life is in reality. The friends have whitewashed the truth to protect God from the charge of presiding over such a blatant miscarriage of justice (13:4, 7-8). As I was writing these words, a man told me his story. He had been sexually abused and brought the perpetrator before the courts. With legal wrangling, the case was not heard for many years. In the end it was thrown out on a technicality and the abuser got away. As a result, the man has started drinking again. Drink or drugs can be a great escape from the feelings of abuse, but the relief is only temporary and addiction becomes a problem in its own right. Truly the wicked often prosper and the broken die in pain and loneliness. Job's observations are borne out in many people's lives.

Job Prays But ……

Job will pray but he will not submit. His prayer is dominated by lament. He speaks to God in a way I had become very afraid of. His laments are also directed against his friends. They presumed that Job had sinned and so deserved his suffering - this was their world-view, as we have seen, and they held this view in the face of the facts of the case. It is easier to stay in an entrenched narrow position than face the insecurities of new questions. Job says to his friends:

In truth I have no help in me,
and any resource is driven from me.
"Those who withhold kindness
from a friend forsake the fear of the Almighty."
My companions are treacherous like a torrent-bed,
like freshets that pass away,
that run dark with ice, turbid with melting snow,
In time of heat they disappear:

when it is hot, they vanish from their place.
The caravans turn aside from their course;
they go up into the waste, and perish.
The caravans of Tema look, the travellers of Sheba hope.
They are disappointed because they were confident:
they come there and are confounded.

(6:13-20)

Job complains that now he has no help and feels lost and alone. He tells his friends that those who withhold kindness 'forsake the fear of the Almighty'. The lonely, abused and rejected know that of which Job speaks. I think personally of the lack of help and compassion I experienced in the dark years of my life. My experience has been the experience of many who found no-one to be with them in their pain and loneliness. Job's complaint is that God may desert one (v. 13), but one should be able to count on friends - even if circumstances lead one to come to doubt God. Abuse and rejection lead one to this pass and so-called friends melt away - leaving one feeling alone. Job's friends' loyalty has been as short-lived as a freshet (v. 15), and as disappointing (v. 20). Like caravans in the southern desert who looked for and hoped for water but were disappointed, so Job's disappointment in his friends is measured by the degree of his former confidence in them. I have found in my life that there is much talk of compassion, but in the hour of my deepest need I found none, only further rejection. 1 remember the words of Peter Van Breemen (*As Bread That is Broken)* that to reject someone is tantamount to killing them. This is the form of living death I experienced in the dark years and every so often the darkness surfaces again and I feel enclosed in a deep, dark pit of despair. Praying the biblical laments is one of my first steps in climbing out of this pit.

Job's prayers also express his sense of helplessness in the face of unbearable suffering. In Chapter 3 he complains:

Why did I not die at birth, come forth from the womb and expire?
Why were there knees to receive me, or breasts for me to suck?
Now I would be lying down and quiet:
I would be asleep; then I would be at rest
with kings and counsellors of the earth
who rebuild ruins for themselves,
or with princes who have gold, who fill their houses with silver:

Or why was I not buried like a stillborn child,
like an infant that never sees the light?
There the wicked cease from troubling,
and there the weary at rest.
There the prisoners are at ease together;
they do not hear the voice of the taskmaster.
The small and the great are there,
and the slaves are free from their masters.
"Why is light given to one in misery, and life to the bitter in soul,
who long for death, but it does not come,
and dig for it more than for hidden treasures;
who rejoice exceedingly, and are glad when they find the grave?
Why is light given to one who cannot see the way,
whom God has fenced in?
For my sighing comes like my bread,
and my groanings are poured out like water,
Truly the thing that I fear comes upon me, and what I dread befalls
on me,
I am not at ease, nor am I quiet? I have no rest; but trouble comes.'
(3:11-26)

The whys of v. 11-12 are a wish that his origins had never been. This has been the theme of Chapter 3 up to now. His cry is equivalent to a death wish that he would like to be retroactive. If he had died at birth he would now enjoy the bliss of peace among the dead. For Job, Sheol, the place of the dead, meant gloom, darkness and forgetfulness (cf. Ps 88:11 - 13 and Job 10:21 -22). Fydor Dostoyevsky caught the mood of Job's lament in his character Ivan Karamazov in his magisterial work, *The Brothers Karamazov.* Ivan has tried to integrate untold misery and devotion to God but concludes:

I refuse to accept this world of God's... Please understand it is not God that I do not accept, but the world he has created. I do not accept God's world and I refuse to accept it. (p. 275)

A few scenes later, Ivan carries his resolution a step further. If extreme misfortune is the cost of accommodating oneself to a divine human relationship, then for Ivan this is too high a price to pay. He complains of the suffering of innocent children and wonders what could justify this. He says:

*We cannot afford to pay so much for admission. And
therefore I hasten to return my ticket of admission... It's not God that
I do not accept, Aloysha. I merely most respectfully return him the
ticket.* (p. 287)

Dostoyevsky himself was deeply disturbed by Ivan and the words
he put into his mouth. At the end of Ivan's Parable of the Grand Inquisitor,
Aloysha's answer is to kiss Ivan and try to give his love in the face of his
bitterness. This was also the answer of Christ to the Grand Inquisitor,
whom he kissed. Job and Dostoyevsky catch the mood of those little ones
who have been hurt. In deep despair, life can lose all its flavour and the
temptation to give up and return one's ticket of admission can be very
powerful. It is very common among those who are abused to contemplate
suicide and quite a lot take this course, unmourned and profoundly lonely.
Others try to escape the pain in addictions of various sorts, but the pain
won't go away. It remains just below the surface and at various times rears
its head, driving one further into despair. I know that place too well.

I recall a Kris Kristofferson song when I meet people who live in
the place of darkness. The song is called 'Billy Dee', and it recounts the
death of a friend of his who committed suicide. In the song we are told that
the world Billy found was lonely but not as lonely as the one he had left
behind. His friends missed him. These words have given hope to the lonely
I have met - it helps them see, even if only in a very dim way, that they are
worth something, even though their bad experience makes them think
differently. It is like the kiss of Christ for the Grand Inquisitor and the kiss
of Aloysha for Ivan. Job is given the option to submit to God or be
condemned by his friends. He opts instead to challenge the God whom he
holds responsible and seeks an answer to his questions.

Job longs for death but it does not come (v. 21). All he is left with
are his tears, which have become his daily bread (v. 24). He tells us he is
not at ease, nor is he quiet. He has no rest, only trouble and grief. This is a
place many know. For a while we are shrouded in grief and there appears
to be no light. It is unbearable to face the fact that this is where we are at.
The laments of Job help put words to the experience. To accept that this is
where one is at is a crucial step, as we have seen in healing. Job dares pour
out his grief to one who for now is silent. In 7:6 he tells us:

*'My days are swifter than a
weaver's shuttle,
and come to their end without hope.'*

And this he fears is the lot of humanity in general (7:1-2). This is what Job has to face up to in himself before he can come to healing.

In Chapter 16 we see Job continue his lament against his friends (so-called!) and God. He is not prepared to give up - he is more prepared to give out! He dares bring his plight before God, even though he feels God's absence. There is, in all of Job's laments, a refusal to give in:

Job answered and said: I have heard plenty of this!
Troublesome comforters, all of you!
Is there a limit to your windy words?
What afflicts you that you argue so?
Now I, I could talk like you
If you were in my place.
I could string arguments together against you
And shake my head over you.
I could encourage you with my mouth,
But the consolation of my lips would bring relief.
                    (16:1-5, Norman Habel's translation)

Here Job belittles the arguments of his friends just as they belittled him (see 8:2). Job calls them 'troublesome comforters' (v. 2b). His jibe is an allusion to their appointed role, as friends whose purpose is to comfort and console the afflicted. Now he castigates his friends as comforters who actually cause rather than ease his misery. An example of what Job means is given dramatically in Chapter 22. Here Eliphaz takes it upon himself to list Job's offences:

'Do not think that he reproves you because you are pious,
that on this account he brings you to trial.
No: it is because you are a very wicked man,
and your depravity passes all bounds.
Without due cause you take a brother in pledge,
you strip men of their clothes and leave them naked.
When a man is weary, you give him no water to drink
and you refuse bread to the hungry.
Is the earth, then, the preserve of the strong
and a domain for the favoured few?
Widows you have sent away empty-handed,
Orphans you have struck defenceless.

No wonder that there are pitfalls in your path,
That snares are set to fill you with sudden fear.'
(22.4-10)

These words are nothing but baseless slander. They have no foundation in fact - the very facts of Job's life contradict these words. Eliphaz's words are a result of his own prejudices - if Job is suffering, he must have sinned, and then Eliphaz lists his faults. This is why Job reacts against his friends in Chapter 16. In Chapter 15, Eliphaz told Job that conceiving evil begets sin. In Chapter 22 he fabricates charges against Job to back his claim.

In 16:3 Job describes Eliphaz's words as 'windy'. He echoes Eliphaz's quip that no wise person would articulate knowledge that was mere 'wind' (15:2). Ironically, Elihu later makes a fool of himself by claiming to be filled with a wind (32:8), which would answer all of their questions. (Elihu is a young man who accompanies the three friends and makes a sudden intervention in chapters 32-38.) He is convinced of his own excellence and his arguments. Yet he unwittingly shows his arguments to be full of 'wind' - a very polite way of saying it! All the friends offered were traditional gestures and verbal formulae that were too superficial to handle Job's problems.

Job's complaints against his friends find an echo in my own experience. After the abuse and years of rejection 1 had to face a lack of compassion in those who could have eased my burden. Instead the one abused was the one who suffered even more. Eventually, however, I did find, as I mentioned, compassionate friends. They all had some brokenness in them. I did have to live with much lack of compassion before I met those friends, let me add.

It was Carl Gustav Jung who spoke of the wounded healer. He spoke of how, when people came to see him and express their pain, he would look into himself and see his own woundedness. This would give him an insight into what his clients were saying. (*Memories, Dreams, and Reflection*, p. 156). Those who have had the courage to embrace their brokenness can be sympathetic and compassionate to their brothers and sisters who have similar wounds. The ultimate wounded healer is Jesus, who passed through the same sufferings as we did. Now he is the supreme high priest who intercedes for his brothers and sisters because he knows their pain. As the letter to the Hebrews reminds us:

*Since, therefore, the children share flesh and blood, he himself
likewise shared the same things so that through death he might
destroy the one who has the power of death, that is, the devil, and
free those who all their lives were held in slavery by the fear of
death. For it is clear that he did not come to help angels, but the
descendants of Abraham. Therefore he had to become like his
brothers and sisters in every respect, so that he might be a merciful
and faithful high priest in the service of God, to make a sacrifice of
atonement for the sins of the people. Because he himself was tested
by, what he suffered, he is able to help those who are being tested.*
(Heb 2:14-18)

For many years, however, my experience was the experience of
Job. I felt heavily the lack of compassion and outright rejection when I was
most afflicted. I can empathise with those who feel this way, and I pray for
all those who feel the healing power of compassionate love.

Here Job voices what it means to feel the desertion of those who
could have proved themselves friends:

Complaint Against God as Enemy

*If I speak, my pain is not relieved;
If I desist - what leaves me? He has now really debilitated me.
You have devastated my whole community.
You have shrivelled me up! That is my witness!
My gaunt appearance testifies against me.
With his anger he rends and rages against me;
He slashes at me with his teeth;
My enemy pierces me with his eyes.
They open wide their mouth at me;
With insolence they smite my jaw;
They form a pack against me.
El delivers me over to evil,
And hurls me into the hands of the wicked.
I was at ease, but he smashed and smashed me;
Seized my neck, then bashed and bashed me.
He set me up as his target;
His archers surrounded me.*

He pierced my kidneys without mercy;
He spilled my bile on the ground.
He breached me, breach after breach;
He charged at me like a warrior.
I sewed sackcloth to my skin
And thrust my horn in the dust.
My face is red from weeping;
Death's shadow falls on my eyelids,
Though there is no violence in my hands
And my plea is pure.

(16:6-17)

Job commences his outburst against God and his unwarranted attacks by declaring that verbal outbursts (e.g. 10:1) or periods of silence (e.g. 2:13) offer no comfort. His bed, too, offers no consolation (7:13) and his friends only intensify his troubles with their verbosity. The real culprit for Job is God. He has reduced Job to an emaciated wreck tortured with pain. Job is alone in his misery. Job's experience expresses the feelings many of us experience in that horrible moment of rejection. Loneliness is the only guest in our house.

In verse 8 Job accuses God of having made him into a pathetic shrivelled wretch who has no credibility in the community. Experiences of illness and depression make one feel as if one is a total outsider - indeed many people do shun a distressed person, as many of us can vouch. In Job's previous speech, he uttered the bold wish that God would hide in Sheol until his anger was past. For Job, God's anger functions like a vicious alter ego which renders His opponents limp and helpless. The term anger ('ap) in Hebrew also carries a second meaning of 'nose' or 'snout', an image consistent with the metaphor of a wild beast. This is how Job sees God and the pass he has brought him to. In verse 9 he also says that his enemy pierces him with his eyes. The eye is the symbol of God's surveillance operation against Job and God hounds him to death (cf. 7:4, 10:4, 14,18, 13:27, 14:3).

These images continue in verses 10-11 where Job speaks of a pack of scavengers who attend God's savage raids on his victims and intensify the plight of his prey. After mauling His prey (v. 9), God, the savage beast, leaves his victim for the gathering pack of the wicked and hurls Job, like a piece of meat, helpless into their midst (v. 11). These are bold-words and indeed shocking for many of us who were trained to bury anger and never speak this way. Job's language is the language of hurt emotion - God has not dealt kindly with him and those who would speak in His name abuse and denigrate Job. This leads to hurt, expressed in anger, and Job pours out his anger to the one who is silent. He dares trust the all-holy One with his anger.

In verse 12 Job continues his charge against God. He repeats words to emphasise doubly the hammer-blows of rejection. Norman Habel translates the words as 'smashed and smashed' and 'bashed and bashed' (see *Job*, p.272) to reflect the feeling of the original Hebrew. Job says he was hit by a violent fighter while he was 'at ease' minding his own business (cf. 1:1-5). While not at war with God. Abuse comes his way. It is a violent interruption into life. Sexual abuse is like this. Sexuality is an important and sacred part of who we are as people and when this is violated a deep wound is inflicted on the spirit as well as the body. This wound can cause anger to be buried for a time but when it erupts it can be a frightening thing. Victims of abuse have an insight into Job's complaints. The last line of verse 12 changes the imagery from God as a fierce fighter to God as the commander directing his army of archers to shoot against Job. The waves of hurt, anger and depression are like arrows in the spirit from the hand of one who abuses. In verse14 Job pictures himself as a fortress wall which God breaks at several points. His forces break down Job's defences and penetrate his inner world. There is no peace, only loneliness. In verse 15 Job's condition is utterly pathetic. He wears sackcloth next to his skin like a person in mourning. He is like one lamenting a death with eyes raw from weeping and surrounded by dark ominous rings (v. 16). The waves of tears that attack the profoundly distressed and depressed can testify to the reality of Job's description of 'eyes ran from tears'. Job cries out that he is guilty of no sin that is worth such humiliation.

The innocent who suffer, like children abused, cry out with the same voice. They carry the wound of the spirit deep into adulthood and may find themselves living with a deep despair and profound loneliness. They cry out with Job that they have committed no sin that is worth such a punishment. Job maintains that in spite of the violence God exhibited as a wild beast and warrior, Job has not retaliated in kind. Job's cry is a formal plea in a forensic sense of a right to be heard, a plea for a legal hearing. When I read this part of Job I think of those who weep and those who weep with those who weep. I will share with you something of my vision. The cry of those abused and such people as parents, friends and loved ones who 'weep with those who weep' is one that demands a hearing in God's

Church. The Church can only move on to become once again what it was called to be when the voices of those it has hurt are heard and accepted as the voices of those who authentically want to be part of the church. I have met many people who are in this hurt place but for the moment they feel like outsiders, that they are not heard or valued. Like Job, there is 'no violence in their hearts and their plea is pure' (v. 17). Only when these lost voices are heard and their story told can we become whole.

Cry of Hope Amid Despair

> *O Earth, cover not my blood*
> *And let my cry have no place.*
> *Surely now my witness is in heaven,*
> *He who can testify for me is on high.*
> *Let him be my advocate, my friend before Eloah,*
> *When my eye weeps in his presence.*
> *Let him arbitrate between a mortal and Eloah*
> *As between one human being and another.*
> *For a few years will pass*
> *And I shall go the way of no return.*
> *My spirit is broken,*
> *My days are spent.*
> *It is the grave for me!*

(16:18-17:2)

In his previous flight of hope Job had dreamed of asylum in Sheol followed by a time for post-mortem litigation and vindication (14:13-17). Now he envisages a new scenario; the blood which was shed in cruel acts of violence will cry out for vindication like the spilled blood of Abel (Gen 4:10). This cry will wander homeless until it is heard by a witness on high. It seems clear from verse 22 that Job hopes his heavenly witness and advocate will take up his cause before his imminent death. God's savage attacks on Job are tantamount to murder. In verse 19-21 we wrestle with the idea of who this heavenly witness is. It could be God Himself since He is the one who avenges innocent blood (cf. Gen. 4:8-12, Is 26:21, Ezek 24:6-9). Gordis argues that behind the God of violence so tragically manifest in the world stands the God of righteousness and love - they are not two but one. (Gordis, *Book of Job*, p. 527, n.15). This, however, according to Habel, goes against the explicit statement of the text. A third mysterious party is being described. Job foresees his celestial witness as one on high who recognises the legitimacy of his cry and is therefore responsible for bringing his case to court. Moreover, in this trial the witness will seem as the arbiter to guarantee due legal process for Job, who envisages putting God in the dock and proving his innocence. There is still hope in Job - even if a somewhat impossible hope in some mysterious stranger! He trusts in the mysterious kindness of strangers - like Blanche at the end of *A Streetcar Named Desire*. He trusts in the mercy of strangers.

In 16.22 Job believes his witness is in heaven and he awaits confirmation of his belief. Soon it will be too late for he will be walking the way-of-no-return (cf. 10:21) to the land of the dead. He already faces the grave with his days spent and his spirit crushed. His hopes have been dashed and his future is beyond redemption. Job is caught in the midst of volcanic emotions. He places his hope, in spite of all that is against him, in some mysterious stranger. There is a refusal in Job to give in, he clings on to any crumb of comfort. His story is repeated many times in many ways. When we are hurt and are trying to cope we become the victims of many emotions, most of them contradictory. Indeed, in writing these meditations I have become more aware of how harrowing and contradictory so many of my own hurt emotions are. The different contradictions and change in moods in the psalms and Job reflect the reality of conflicting and contradictory emotions. The emotional life does not admit of pure logic. To bear this out, at the end of Job's speech in chapter 17 he is once again down in the dumps. The momentary high of 16:18-17:1 is now replaced by despair. This is Job's world of volcanic emotions.

Cry of Despair About Hope

My days are done,
My schemes are severed,
All the desires of my heart
That would turn night into day
And keep light near in the face of darkness.
If I must hope for Sheol as my home,
Spread my couch in darkness,
Call out to the Pit, "You are my Father!"
To the worm, "My Mother!" "My Sister!"
Where then is my hope?
My hope, who can see it?

Will it descend to Sheol?
Shall we go down to the dust together?

(17:11-16)

This section comes immediately after Job's further complaints against his so-called friends (17:2-10). After his sudden flight into hope he finds himself once again in the depths and facing despair. In her study of death and dying, Elizabeth Kubler-Ross showed that as we try to come to terms with dying, we go through a variety of stages and emotions. Walter Brueggemann speaks of the psalms of lament. These belong to the period of disorientation we feel, when our old familiar world is shattered (see Message of the Psalms}. This shows that in the emotional world we are subject to volatile emotions as we try to come to terms with grief and trauma. This is what Job reflects on in these passages. He is at one moment relatively upbeat, then some minutes later he is depressed. Real life doesn't make sense. Life is stranger than fiction because fiction, after all, must make sense. This experience of conflicting emotions and moods is something I noticed in myself in my own periods of disorientation.

In 17:11-12 Job opens his speech with an outburst of frustration that his life is terminating without any of his hopes being realised (v. 11). He had hope that his life would be acquitted before a tribunal where he could present his case free from intimidation or duplicity. That hope, he had declared, would sustain him even if his trial were held after a period of asylum in Sheol (14:13-17). Here he describes the hope in his heart as an expectation that the night of his despair will turn to day and that a light will shine in the darkness of his misery (v. 12). In the following speech Bildad twists the language of Job's hope, asserting that the light of the wicked eventually fades (18:5-6).

In verses13-14 Job takes up the theme of Sheol as a home where he makes his bed and treats his companions as members of his family with the pit as his father and the worm as his mother/sister. The pit refers to the underworld as the domain of corruption, filth and the fallen (see 9:3, 33: 38). The worm is likewise a symbol of decay and death (see 7:5, 21:26).

In verses15-16 the closing cries of this speech raise once again the question of death as an unjust termination point for mortal hope (cf. 16:22). His dreams of asylum are over, now he cries out in frustration. What will happen to this life of vindication when he dies? Is this the end of it all? Is there still some faltering hope even in Sheol?

These reflections of Job catch the mood of despair of those who suffer with no-one to hear them. Often they take their lives, sonic times by suicide or by succumbing to a broken heart. Saul Bellow entitled one of his works More Die of Heartbreak. They die unmourned and the world doesn't note their passing. There are many victims of abuse who have come to that pass while those who destroyed them live on without one thought for those they have hurl. Job's words are bitter and harrowing. I taste the bitterness in ins mouth as I read them and all I can do is offer a prayer to God for those whose lives are burdensome and who are alone. After all, this is what Job was doing... He teaches us that we are not alone.

Job never doubted the existence, the power or the omnipotence of God but he is driven to wonder if he is merely a plaything in (he hands of a capricious God who forever eludes his grasp, and w host-ways he can neither understand nor justify. He never ceases lo reach out, pour out his lament to the one who remains elusive. He says:

If only I knew how to find him,
how to enter his court,
I would state my case before him
and set out my arguments in full.
Then I should learn what answer he would give
and find out what he had to say.
Would he exert his great power to browbeat me?
No; God himself would never bring a charge against me.
There the upright are vindicated before him,
and I shall win from my judge an absolute discharge.
If I go forward, he is not there;
if backward, I cannot find him; when I turn left, I do not descry him;
1 face right, but 1 see him not.

(23.2-9)

The stage is now set for the next scene in the dramatised lament. In the lament the complaint is poured out to God and there is an act of faith that God hears and enters the scene.

From the Whirlwind

Then the LORD answered Job out of the whirlwind:
'Who is this that darkens counsel by words without knowledge?

Gird up your loins like a man. I will question you,
and you shall declare to me.
'Where were you when I laid the foundation of the earth?"
Tell me, if you have understanding.
Who determined its measurements - surely you know!
Or who stretched the line upon it?
On what were its bases sunk,
or who laid its cornerstone when the morning stars sang together
and all the heavenly beings shouted for joy?

(Job 38:1:-7)

Suddenly in the drama comes a storm. We are told the Lord spoke to Job from the whirlwind. Up to this point, the names used for God have been El, Eloah, El Shaddai but now Yahweh ('Lord') is the name used. Yahweh is the God of Moses, Jacob and Isaac, the one who spoke to Moses on the mountain.

Severe storms, though relatively rare in Palestine, were associated with theophanies of Yahweh from Israel's earliest history (Ex 19:9-20, Judg 5:4-5, Heb 3:5-6, Ps 18:8-16). Yahweh s answer to Job is like his answer to Moses in the thunder of Sinai (Ex 19:9), when Yahweh revealed himself in visible form to the people, as a cloud by day, a pillar by night. Yet is it fair to say that God answers Job? The answer of Yahweh, unlike those of the friends, gives no reason for Job's sufferings. It is as though those sufferings are left enshrouded in the mystery of their givenness, their having happened. There are two sets of Yahweh s answers to Job (38:1-40:2; 40:6-42-34).

All God does is to deny Job's charges of dark purpose and indifference to justice and to ask Job these sorts of questions: 'Who are you? Where were you? Are you able?' On the face of it these questions are rhetorical and have the specific force of asking questions to which the proper answers are: I am nothing, I was not there and I am not able. J. Gerald Janzen, however, points out that these apparently rhetorical questions are to be taken ironically, as veiling existential questions posed to Job (J. Gerald Janzen, *Job*, p. 225).

The questions, as from another burning bush, has to do with the issue of Job's willingness to enter into God, into the human vocation of royal rule in the image of God, when the implications of that image are intimated in terms of innocent suffering.

Wayne Booth sees irony as having the function of subverting the very view it seems to affirm, in order to establish the very view to which the hearer or the reader is invited (*A Rhetoric of Irony*, p. 1). Janzen uses this argument to contend that the divided speech, while appearing to reaffirm certain kinds of conventional wisdoms concerning creativity and creatureliness, and the wisdoms appropriate to them, in fact speaks of a deeper wisdom in the understanding of humankind as the divine image. Job and the reader are invited to a new mode of participation in the realities of creatureliness and creativity, light and darkness, (*Job*, p. 226).

I find Janzen's arguments convincing. In 42:7, Yahweh tells us that Job spoke well of him while the friends did not. So the suggestion that God is reaffirming old wisdoms is contradicted here. At one time on a superficial level when I first read the statements and questions of God to Job, I had the impression that God was trying to crush Job. In the voice of Yahweh, I could hear the voice of my own fears. They remind me of all the harsh words and brow-beating I went through, especially after the abuse I suffered. I found no compassion, only its polar opposite. Perhaps I thought when I read this chapter that this was what God was like after all. Yet at the conclusion of the book, Job and God are friends. Job is not browbeaten but is at peace with God. This edges me towards accepting Jazen's view of the divine speeches. Job surrenders to love and prays for all those who are in distress (including his three friends) that they come to share in that love. The answers to the why of innocent suffering aren't given but the facile arguments of the friends are rejected and suffering, especially innocent suffering, is left wrapped in mystery, but now with the important addition that Yahweh does care and is with the sufferer.

Job 42:1-6 is difficult to translate from the Hebrew (see Habel, *Job, p.* 376f). Gustavo Guttierrez offers the following translation (*On Job*, p. 83):

> *This was the answer Job gave to Yahweh:*
> *I know that you are all-powerful and there is no plan you cannot carry out.*
> *(You said:) "Who is this that blurs my plans with ignorant words?"*
> *- It is true: I spoke without understanding*
> *marvels that are beyond my grasp.*
> *(You said:) "Listen to me, for I am going to speak;*
> *I am going to ask the questions, and you are to inform me."*
> *I once knew you only by hearsay, now my eyes have seen you;*
> *therefore I repudiate and repent of dust and ashes*

[42:1-6]

There are three steps in this response of Job. There is an acknowledgement that God has plans and that these are being carried out. There is also a discovery of unrecognised aspects of reality, and a joyous encounter with the Lord, whom Job has discovered. This leads Job from the place of sadness and complaint. It is the third step.

This reading of Job ties in with the idea of Job as a dramatised lament. In the lament psalm it begins with sadness, complaint and lament but there is also faith that through the words God is present and enters the situation. Psalm 22 is an example of this. It begins with the words, 'My God, my God, why have you forsaken me?' This could easily be the prayer of Job - it was the prayer of Jesus. In Psalm 22 the psalmist feels like a worm scorned and despised by everyone (v.6). God is far away (v.11); only trouble and distress are at hand.

The imagery shifts in verses 12-21 to provide a terrifying description of the trouble. The complaints are populated by animals that surround the psalmist. The following words convey the bad shape the psalmist is in:

> *Many bulls encircle me,*
> *strong bulls of Bashan*
> *surround me;*
> *they open wide their mouths at me,*
> *like a ravening and roaring lion.*
> *I am poured out like water,*
> *and all my bones are out of joint;*
> *my heart is like wax;*
> *it is melted within my breast:*
> *my mouth is dried up like a potsherd*
> *and my tongue sticks to my jaws;*
> *you lay me in the dust of death.*
> *For dogs are all around me:*
> *a company of evildoers*
> *encircles me.*
> *My hands and feet have shrivelled;*
> *I can count all my bones.*
> *They stare and gloat over me;*
> *they divide my clothes among themselves,*
> *and for my clothing they cast lots.*
> *But you, O LORD, do not be far away!*

O my help, come quickly to my aid!
Deliver my soul from the sword,
my life from the power of the dog!
Save me from the mouth of the lion.

(Ps 22:12-21)

Like the first major section of the psalm, the second ends with a plea that both reintroduces the cast of animals, who symbolise and dramatise the state of the psalmist, and provides a link to the first plea by way of repetition of 'for' and 'help' (v. 19; see v. 11). The psalmist is utterly dehumanised, but something is changing. Whereas the psalmist concluded there was no help in verse 11, here he addresses God as 'my help'. Translating verse 21b literally, it says: 'From the horns of the wild oxen you have answered me', (see J. Clinton McCann, *A Theological Introduction to the Book of Psalms*, p. 171). The opening complaint of the psalm has been reversed: God has answered, but the answer comes not from beyond the suffering but precisely in its midst. God is present in the depths and even in death. He is present in apparent God-forsakenness

The pattern of Psalm 22 and many other laments help show us how Job is a dramatised lament. Job doesn't get answers but is led into a new union of love with God when freedom addresses freedom.

The final speech as we have it in the book of Job goes to God. He addresses Eliphaz with the following words:

> *My wrath is kindled against you and against your two friends; for you have not spoken truth [nekonah] of me as my servant Job has. Now therefore take seven bulls and seven rams, and go to my servant Job, and offer up for yourselves a burnt offering: and my servant Job will pray for you [yitpallel alekem] for I will accept his prayer [lit. 'lift up the face'] not to do folly with you: for you have not spoken truth [nekonah] of me as my servant Job has. "So Eliphaz the Temanite and Bildad the Shuhite and Zophar the Naamathite went and did what the LORD had told them; and the LORD accepted Job's prayer [lit. "lifted up the face"]. (42:7-9)*
> (Balentine, *Prayer, p. 182).*

Here Job is affirmed as one who has spoken truly and whose prayers God will accept on behalf of others. One could argue that the whole of the book has been oriented towards this end (Balentine, *Prayer*, p. 182).

Job had requested justice, he has been granted communion (cf. 42:5: 'now my eye sees you'). It is important, according to W. Lee Humphreys, to recognise that such an experience of God takes place in the struggle with pain and suffering (*Tragic Vision*, p. 116). The one who dares to speak, to lament, to complain in the presence of God is now invited into an intimacy with God. It is not the friends who merely parrot answers without understanding the questions, where prayers are heard. It is Job who has wrestled with God, complained and come to silence where prayers are heard. On the other side of Job's transferring, his words are transformed and transforming. This happens after the divine speeches. He is the suffering servant who helps bind the wounds of those who suffer.

Can I leave Job there? There is still one further question that was with me when I read the conclusion of Job for the first time. Is the end of Job too much for us to hope for? There is another book called Ecclesiastes (or Qoheleth), in which Qoheleth complains that God is in heaven and we are on earth (Ecc 5:2). This suggests a chasm between us and God, and our two worlds do not meet. Qoheleth is melancholic but his statements flesh out my greatest fear... Is God for us? Or is the vision of Job just a dream, meant for others but not for me? It is to these questions I now turn for a moment.

How else but through a broken heart?

When I look at the questions I asked above, I become aware of when the questions surfaced. They are the voice of my fear and anxiety. True and perfect love can drive out fear (1 Jn. 4:18) but 1 am also sure that perfect fear can drive out love, leaving one locked in a lonely world, not daring to trust. I knew that place. After the incident of abuse, I received no support, only further rejection and this has left me with a legacy of fear. When the anxiety overcomes me, as it often does, I find it hard to keep on going. This is a profoundly lonely world, and realisation of this helps me understand why I had so many questions at the end of reading Job. The book of Job was a deep consolation in my loneliness. In one of his poems, *'Loneliness'*, W.H. Auden captures what it means to be in such a lonely world:

> *Gate-crashing ghost, aggressive*
> *invisible visitor,*
> *tactless gooseberry, spoiling*

my tete-a-tete with myself,
blackmailing brute, behaving
as if the house were your own,
so viciously pursuing
your victim from room to room,
monotonously nagging, ungenerous jabberer,
dirty devil, befouling
fair fancies, making the mind
a quagmire of disquiet,
weakening my will to work,
shadow without shape or sex,
excluding consolation,
blotting out Nature s beauties,
grey mist between me and God,
pestilent problem that won't
be put on the back-burner,
hard it is to endure you.

(W.H. Auden, *Collected Poems*, p. 866)

The gate-crashing ghost of loneliness is the aggressive visitor who haunts me.

Thoughts, harsh-words that cut, break in uninvited and for a while convince one that they are the only reality. They behave indeed as if the house of myself was their own and nobody else's. They make the mind 'a quagmire of disquiet', making living a burden. Fear and loneliness can blind me to beauty and put a 'grey mist' before me and God.

I stayed in this condition for many years, and once again it was a compassionate friend who appeared in the midst of my darkness. I was stationed in a place where I did not feel at home or welcome, but I thought I had kept this from the people I served. However, one couple sensed my loneliness and Angela, the wife, gently suggested I read Nikos Kazantzakis's *Report to Greco*. How well people know us in spite of ourselves!

This restless Cretan spoke to me in many passages of his book, though one in particular stands out. It was this:

> *One of the apocryphal Gospels relates how the beloved disciple John had an astounding vision as he stood weeping before the Crucified. The cross was not of wood but of light, and crucified*

upon it was not a single man but rather thousands of men, women and children, all groaning and dying. The beloved disciple trembled, unable to capture and immobilise any of the innumerable figures. All kept changing, running, disappearing; some returned a second time. Suddenly they all vanished and nothing remained on the cross but a crucified Cry.

(Report to Greco, p. 414)

I thought this was one of the most beautiful things I had ever read. God spoke through the person of Jesus. All those who suffer, all the Jobs of this world, are in a profound union with God in Jesus. God is with us in Jesus in our distress and suffers with us. I could at last be at peace with the vision of the dramatist who wrote Job. The cries of all who suffer, Jesus and all his brothers and sisters, everywhere and in every time, form one single crucified cry to God, who hears and leads us to new life. His vision gave me the courage to face my loneliness and fear.

I leave the final word in this chapter to Oscar Wilde. *In The Ballad of Reading Gaol*, Oscar writes the following lines. We are not doomed to eternally hurt one another:

How else but through a broken heart
May Lord Christ enter in?

(Selected Poems, p. 125)

Chapter 6

A Whirlpool of Torment

Psalm 73

Truly God is good to the upright
to those who are pure in heart
But as for me, my feet had almost stumbled;
my steps had nearly slipped.
For I was envious of the arrogant;
I saw the prosperity of the wicked.
For they have no pain;
their bodies are sound and sleek.
They are not in trouble as others are;
they are not plagued like other people.
Therefore pride is their necklace;
violence covers them like a garment.
Their eyes swell out with fatness;
their hearts overflow with follies.
They scoff and speak with malice;
loftily they threaten oppression.
They set their mouths against heaven,
and their tongues range over the earth.

Therefore the people turn and praise them,
and find no fault in them.
And they say, 'How can God know?
Is there knowledge in the Most High?'
Such are the wicked;
always at ease, they increase in riches.
All in vain I have kept my heart clean
and washed my hands in innocence.
For all day long I have been plagued,
and am punished every morning.
If I had said, I will talk on in this way',
I would have been untrue to the circle of your children.
But when I thought how to understand this,
it seemed to me a wearisome task,

until I went into the sanctuary;
then I perceived their end.
Truly you set them in slippery places;
You make them fall to ruin.
How they are destroyed in a moment,
swept away utterly by terrors!
They are like a dream when one awakes;
on awaking you despise their phantoms.

When my soul was embittered,
when I was pricked in heart,
I was stupid and ignorant;
I was like a brute beast towards you.
Nevertheless I am continually with you;
you hold my right hand.
You guide me with your counsel
and afterward you will receive me with honour.
Whom have I in heaven but you?
And there is nothing on earth
that I desire other than you.
My flesh and my heart may fail,
but God is the strength of my heart and my portion forever.

Indeed, those who are far from you will perish;
you put an end to those who are false to you.
But for me it is good to be near God;
I have made the Lord GOD my refuge, to tell of all your works.

Psalm 73 is a psalm with which I can identify. The psalmist is honest with himself and, on the basis of painful personal experience, he faces the question: 'What does it mean to talk about the goodness of God when there is so much in the world which seems in call goodness into question?' I apply it to the situation of loneliness, particularly (but not exclusively) to loneliness arising from rejection and abuse. By observation I can see that the victims suffer while the perpetrators are oblivious to their pain and indeed often live lives free from detection. Relatively few abusers are brought to trial and even then the victims have to engage in lengthy legal battles.

I apply Psalm 73 to my loneliness and experiences. It is rooted in the same problem which haunts the book of Job (e.g. the conflicting arguments of Zophar and Job in chapters 20 and 21). Life doesn't hand down the script which much traditional theological thinking has handed down. The script is encapsulated in the words of Isaiah 48:22, 'There is no peace,' says the Lord, 'for the wicked'. But the psalmist in Psalm 73 protests: 'I saw the prosperity of the wicked' (v. 3). The word used in Isaiah 48:22 for peace and in Psalm 73:3 for prosperity is shalom.

This Hebrew word is rich in meaning and there is no one English word that is adequate to translate it. Shalom points to life in its fullness and the person with shalom has peace, health, joy and prosperity. This is the meaning of the blessing in Psalm 29:11.

Psalm 73 was also Martin Buber's favourite psalm (see *Buber*, 45-65, p. 409-411) It's influence can be seen in this poem:

A strange (loud) voice speaks:
A rope is stretched across the abyss,
Now set your foot on it
And, before your step awakens the contradiction,
Run!
A rope is tightly strung across the abyss,
Renounce on the way all that is here!
Already there beckons to you from over there a hand:
'To me!'

Follow not the demanding call!
He who created you
Intended for you: 'Be ready
For every earthly time!'
Already his hand ever holds you -
Remain turned toward the world in love!

This shows Buber's openness to the Spirit and it also shows that his experience leads him in active engagement to heal the world.

The sentence of the second stanza, 'Already his hand ever holds you', is an unmistakable reference to Psalm 73:

And nevertheless I am always with you,
You have taken hold of my right hand.

You guide me with your counsel
And afterward you take me into honour.

It was this psalm that Buber read at Franz Rosenweig's funeral and it was those four lines that were inserted on Buber's tombstone at his own request. Psalm 73 embodies Buber's deepest attitude towards death. Buber wrote an essay on Psalm 73, entitled *'The Heart Determines'*. As this title shows, it is the state of the heart that determines the nearness to God of the man who is 'pure in heart' and the 'nothingness' in which the wicked end up - the 'impure of heart'. Those who use, exploit and pursue others end up cutting themselves off from the love they crave and never become authentic human beings. What is remarkable about Psalm 73, for Buber, is that the psalmist tells how he recalled the true meaning of his experience of life, and that this meaning borders directly on the eternal. We cannot penetrate to the heart of the mysteries of our experiences of life. It requires a deeper experience of the Presence of God to do this.

Insofar as the psalmist becomes pure in heart, he experiences God's goodness, not as some reward, but as the revelation of what he cannot know from his side of the dialogue - that he is continually with God. This is not a final conclusion. Buber cautioned: 'From man's side there is no continuity of presence, only from God's side'. He can only see that in the revelation, God is continually with him—this is known in a gesture, that God has taken his right hand.

Despite all his own personal experience of the prosperity of the wicked of which Psalm 73 speaks, Buber compared this to the way in which a father takes his little child by the hand in the dark, in order to partially lead the child, 'but primarily in order to make present to him, in the warm touch of his coursing blood, the fact that he, the Father, is continually with him'. The moment Buber points out in Psalm 73 is one many of us encounter on the journey we are making. His experiences of the wicked who prosper and the good who suffer is very real for many - for a time even more real than the revelation of the hand of God guiding us. We must journey in the psalm to reach this place, and the heart determines the way we approach this journey. Honesty and sincerity are the ways we prepare for God to enter.

Buber reflects also on death and his attitude in the light of being in the presence of God:

'For the "oppressed" man death was only the mouth towards which the sluggish stream of suffering and trouble flows.

But now it has become the event in which God — the continually Present One, the One who grasps the man's hand, the Good One - "takes" a man.'

On one hand there is nothing in Psalm 73 that speaks about being able to enter heaven after death. Buber claimed 'As far as I see, there is nowhere in the Old Testament anything about this'. The honour into which one is afterward taken is not some glorious afterlife but rather, from the human point of view, the fulfilment of existence; and from God's point of view, the entrance into God's eternity.

Buber states:
'It is not merely his flesh which vanishes in death, but also his heart, that inmost personal organ of the soul, which formerly "rose up" in rebellion against the human fate and which he then "purified" till he became pure in heart - this personal soul also vanishes. But He who was the true part and true fate of this person, the 'rock' of his heart. God, is eternal. It is into His eternity that he who is pure in heart moves in death, and this eternity is something absolutely different from any kind of time.' (p. 210)

In the end, however, the dynamic of being far away and being near for God is broken by death when it breaks the life of the person. For the Christian, the grasp of God's hand is something that is eternal. It starts now and is caught up into eternity. As 1 John puts it, our faith rests on the fact, not that we loved God but that God loved us and sent us his son...' (1 Jn. 4:10). It is something that takes our step beyond the psalmist's vision, since this son is the 'Christ who has been raised from the dead, the first fruits of those who have died' (1 Cor. 15:20). He is the destroyer of the last enemy death (1 Cor. 15:24). We now share in his spirit. Psalm 73 prepares the way for this vision.

Now let us enter into Psalm 73 and pray that we experience the healing presence of which Buber speaks.

Psalm 73 begins with the line: 'Truly God is good to the upright, to those who are pure in heart.' In the first verses the names used for God are El and Elohim. Later on in the psalm the more personal name Yahweh is given to God as the psalmist moves closer to a relationship with Him. This is similar to Job: we saw the same movement in the book of Job - from the more impersonal name to the more personal Yahweh. This gives us a hint that in Psalm 73 not everything is as it should be at the start. The verse gives the starting point for the psalmist's problem since it expresses traditional teaching that bitter experience had led the psalmist to question.

Bitter experience has led many of us to question what was handed down unquestioningly. My own experience in trying to come to God was marked by rejection and ultimately abuse. There were many questions and hurt emotions locked inside. This was not just my experience but the experience of many. I think of those whose children were abused by ministers of the church. These people believed in God and trusted his representatives. They are left with the question: how could this happen to those who trusted God or his representatives? There are many more victims of those who were betrayed by loved ones, people whom they trusted. Their stories comprise the majority of abuse reports, but they aren't given the same prominence as abuse by ministers of the gospel. This does not mean that their pain is any less. Bitter experience had led many of us to wince at statements such as verse 1 of Psalm 73. The same inner conflict was in the psalmist and in many writers of the Old Testament.

Gerard Manley Hopkins was a Jesuit priest who experienced deep loneliness in his ministry and life. He was a very sensitive soul and his sensitivity made him become more and more isolated. From this loneliness he produced some lovely poetry. In the following poem he pours out his loneliness and how distant from God this makes him feel:

> *I WAKE and feel the fell of dark, not day.*
> *What hours, O what black hours we have spent*
> *This night! what sights you, heart, saw; ways you went!*
> *And more must, in yet longer light's delay.*
> *With witness I speak this.   But where I say*
> *Hours 1 mean years, mean life. And my lament*
> *Is cries countless, cries like dead letters sent*
> *To dearest him that lives alas! away.*
>
> *I am gall, I am heartburn.   God's most deep decree*
> *Bitter would have me taste: my taste was me;*
> *Bones built in me, flesh filled, blood brimmed the curse.*
> *Selfyeast of spirit a dull dough sours. I see*
> *The lost are like this, and their scourge to be*
> *As I am mine, their sweating selves; but worse.*

'I wake and feel the fell of dark, not day.' Hopkins makes us feel as if an oppressive weight has been thrown on him, as in the Plague of Egypt, a darkness that can be felt. The plague of spiritual darkness spreads all over the poet. It colours time, for the hours become black hours, and it disfigures the part as the hours are interpreted as years. In re-traversing the past the poet is unable to forgive himself for well-meant blunders. His lament takes the form of 'cries countless', like 'dead letters' sent to the one who seems so far distant. The letters are 'dead' because his cries remain unanswered. Guilt over mistakes, 'dead letters' and 'cries countless' are things I remember from my hours of deep melancholy. I felt my fears and cries were useless and unheard - confirming my negative view of myself.

In the next stanza of the poem the emergency becomes medical. During severe jaundice, the gall or bile, whose function is to help us digest nourishment, seems instead to permeate the whole system, flooding into the blood and the lymph, stirring the tissue and skin and eyes until the victim feels 'I am gall'. Instead of being nourished by bread, he is being nauseated by a 'dull dough' soured by 'selfyeast' and bile, and the sweating points to a feverish hepatitis. The diet, like the darkness, is not due to any conscious choice on his part. He is not a prodigal son, but a dutiful if imperfect one, whom the father he loves has apparently deserted without explanation. The punishment and pain are out of proportion to the shortcomings of the poet - echoes of Job. Hopkins, explains, 'God would have me taste his deep bitter decree'.

Hopkins echoes Psalm 42, which has the following lines:

My tears have been my food day and night,
while people say to me continually: where is Your God? (v. 3)

This sonnet of Hopkins ends somewhat enigmatically, perhaps because he could not decide whether it was more painful to be an outlaw, aware that he is unjustly punished, or be a loyal citizen summarily imprisoned on an unknown charge and left to languish unheard. Kafka caught the same mood in his work *The Trial*. Joseph K., the main character, is charged with some grave crime, the nature of which he does not know, and he feels oppressed under the weight of the trial against him. Hopkins complains that the fate of the lost is just like his and their scourge is to be 'to be as I am mine'. However he admits he must still at least have hope.

Jeremiah was a discouraged prophet who experienced much agony in his service of God. Within the present form of the book of Jeremiah, there are a series of passages which have been varyingly called his confessions, his 'personal diary', and his 'laments and complaints'. Although voices have been raised, suggesting that these complaints are liturgical and are late additions that tell us nothing of Jeremiah's inner struggle, I side with John Bright who says that however much these passages employ conventional, cultic forms and language such as we find in the psalms of lament, we are forced to see behind the conventional forms a prophetic individual persecuted because of the word, suffering mental and physical anguish, and lashing out at his persecutors - and God! (*Jeremiah's Complaints*, p. 190). Hopkins expressed his own battle, which could just as easily apply to Jeremiah.

> *'A warfare of my lips in truth;*
> *Battling with God is now my prayer.'*

In Jeremiah 12: 1-2, Jeremiah faces his bitter experience and turns to God and complains:

> *You will be in the right.*
> *O LORD,*
> *when I lay charges against you;*
> *but let me put my case to you.*
> *Why does the way of the guilty prosper?*
> *Why do all who are*
> *treacherous thrive?*
> *You plant them, and they take root;*
> *They grow and bring forth fruit:*
> *you are near in their mouths*
> *yet far from their hearts.*

Jeremiah sets out this complaint in a legal form, as if he is trying to bring God to trial. His charge is that the guilty prosper and the treacherous thrive. They use the name of God but they are far from him in their hearts. Yet the one who suffers is Jeremiah.

In 20:14-18, we see Jeremiah still in the grip of the same mood of deep personal despondency. The dark shadow of failure and rejection has blighted his life. The curse he shouts out here is much more violent than any found in the psalms of lament:

Cursed be the day
on which I was born!
The day when my mother bore me
let it not be blessed!
Cursed be the man
who brought the news to my father, saying,
'A child is born to you, a son,'
making him very glad.
Let that man be like the cities
that the LORD overthrew
without pity;
let him hear a cry in the morning
and an alarm at noon.
because he did not kill me in the womb;
so my mother would have
been my grave,
and her womb forever great.
Why did I come forth from the womb
to see toil and sorrow,
and spend my days in shame?

(Jer. 20:14-18)

This 'before-birth-death-wish' is very uncharacteristic of the Old Testament. Life comes as God's gift, a gift to be enjoyed and lived to the full. Even the author of Psalm 22 in the dark night of his soul, surrounded by rejection, scorn and abuse, draws strength from remembering:

'Yet it was you who took me from the womb;
You have kept me safe on my mother's breast
On you I was cast from my birth,
and since my mother bore me you have been my God.'

(Ps 22:9-10)

The only parallel to Jeremiah's cry is to be found in Job 3, which may have been influenced by Jeremiah's words. The spirit of these words is a wish to have never been. He is lonely, feels abused and that all he does is a waste. Life had become a burden too heavy to bear. Jeremiah cries out:

'Why is my pain unceasing, my wound incurable, refusing to be healed?'

(15:18)

The most shocking of Jeremiah's reproaches and complaints is against God and is found in 20:7-8. He lashes out, saying:

You have seduced me, Yahweh,
and I have let myself be seduced;
you have overpowered me:
you were the stronger.
I am a laughing-stock all day long,
they all make fun of me.
For whenever I speak, I have to howl
and proclaim, 'Violence and ruin!'
For me, Yahweh s word has been the cause
of insult and derision all day long.

In 20:7, quoted above, Jeremiah accuses God of rape. This is no trivial accusation, nor is it uttered in a flippant manner. The words are carefully chosen to illustrate how Jeremiah feels. In this charge, Jeremiah, who was called to be celibate by God (16:1-4), now feels himself violated by the one he loves. He felt helpless before God's words and was therefore overwhelmed. To describe what has happened to him, Jeremiah can think of no more apt image than seduction and rape.

Victims of abuse can relate to the shock of Jeremiah's words. Indeed, in many victims there is a feeling of resentment against God and anybody who could have helped. Why did God allow this? Many parents of children who have been abused suffer hostility from their children because deep down the child feels the parent should somehow have protected him or her. Here we are dealing with the field of hurt emotions and not hard logic. In Jeremiah's case, after his feeling of abuse, he has to face the laughter, derision and rejection of those who see his plight.

In the beginning, Yahweh's words for Jeremiah were a source of sheer joy:

Your words were found, and I ate them,
and your words became to me a joy
and the delight of my heart;
for I am called by your name,
O LORD, God of hosts.

(Jer. 15:16)

From this description we see how influential God's words were. Now Jeremiah has to face the cold reality of rejection and perceived abuse. This is the journey the psalmist is on in Psalm 73. I am on this journey also.

Reality Bites

In the next part of Psalm 73, the psalmist looks at bitter reality and places that in confrontation with his previous faith (v. 1) He is someone with one foot in the temple, where he shares the prayers of his people, and the other foot is in the camp of the wisdom schools who look at reality and place their faith and theology in confrontation with the reality of experience. Psalm 73 continues with the following lines:

But as for me, my feet had
almost stumbled;
my steps had nearly slipped.
For I was envious of the arrogant;
I saw the prosperity of the wicked.

For they have no pain;
their bodies are sound and sleek.
They are not troubled as others are;
they are not plagued like other people.
Therefore pride is their necklace;
violence covers them like a garment.
Their eyes swell out with fatness;
their hearts overflow with follies.
They scoff and speak with malice;
loftily they threaten oppression.

They set their mouths against heaven,
and their tongues range over the earth.

Therefore the people turn and praise them,
and find no fault in them.
And they say, 'How can God know?
Is there knowledge in the Most High?'
Such are the wicked;
always at ease, they increase in riches.
All in vain I have kept my heart clean
and washed my hands in innocence.
For all day long I have been plagued,
and am punished every morning.

(Ps 73:2-14)

Verses 2-3 lay bare the problem that has taken the psalmist to within an inch of losing his grip and the faith that had hitherto given him security. He is wrestling with real doubts that will not go away. The 'prosperity of the wicked' (v. 3) is what sparked off his doubt, but he is honest enough to admit there is another factor. He begrudges the wicked their success. He is envious of the arrogant and boastful. When one is down it is hard not to begrudge those who do evil and thrive. In cases of abuse, the abused feel deep wounds in their hearts while those who abuse often seem to do well. Indeed, when you are down, it is easy to imagine that everyone else is doing well.

The Book of Proverbs may warn: 'Do not let your heart envy sinners, but always continue in the fear of the Lord' (Prob. 23:17); but when sinners seem to be rewarded handsomely and those who fear the Lord suffer pain and rejection, envy is something that is hard to avoid.

Psalm 73 began with the same promise as Psalm 1, which asserted faith in a naturally coherent universe. Psalm 1 says that they are happy who delight in the law of the Lord. It says of the good:

They are like trees
planted by streams of water,
which yield their fruit in its season,
and their leaves do not wither.
In all that they do, they prosper.

(Ps 1:3)

The good are rewarded while:

> *The wicked are not so,*
> *but are like chaff that the wind*
> *drives away.*
> *Therefore the wicked will not*
> *stand in judgment.*
> *- nor sinners in the congregation*
> *of the righteous:*
> *for the LORD watches over*
> *the way of the righteous,*
> *but the way of the wicked will perish.*

> (1:4-6)

The writer of Psalm 73 protests against such a worldview. The promise of Psalm 1 and Psalm 73:1 is not reliable. The psalmist in 73 observes that the wicked, the same wicked portrayed in Psalm 1 as chaff, do very well and do not perish. He observes:

> *For they have no pain;*
> *their bodies are sound and sleek*
> *They are not in trouble as others are;*
> *They are not plagued like other people.*
> *Therefore pride is their necklace;*
> *violence covers them like a garment.*
> *Their eyes swell out with fatness;*
> *their hearts overflow with follies.*
> *They scoff and speak with malice;*
> *loftily they threaten oppression.*
> *They set their mouths against heaven,*
> *and their tongues range over the earth.*

> (Ps 73:2-9)

The wicked enjoy the prosperity that goes with success (v. 10). They are prepared to defy God, assuming that He is some remote distant deity who has no care for his people (v. 11). The wicked are like this, says the psalmist, and their reward is security (v. 12).

The psalmist's reaction, born of envy (v. 3), is that if this is what life is like, what is the point of being committed to the purity and innocence he believes to be part of believing in God'? His reward is 'affliction' - the same word used of the suffering servant in Isaiah 53:4 and of Job in Job 1:11—and 'punishment'. The psalmist is perplexed like Job and Jeremiah.

Like Job and the author of Psalm 73, Qoheleth exhibits dissent from any view that claims the righteous enjoy Shalom, the wicked meet with trouble in life. 'In my earthly existence Qoheleth, 'I have seen it all, from a righteous man perishing in his righteousness to a wicked man growing old in his wickedness' (Ecc 7:15). What happened to the promise of the righteous receiving long life and wickedness leading to a swift and unpleasant end? Nor for Qoheleth is there any relation between merit and success in life:

> One more thing I have observed here under the sun: speed does not win the race, nor strength the battle. Bread does not belong to the wise, nor wealth to the intelligent, nor success to the skilful; time and chance govern all. Moreover no man knows when his hour will come; like fish caught in a net, like a bird taken in a snare, so men are trapped when bad times come suddenly. (9.11-12, cf.9.1-13).

Chapter 8:11-13 in Qoheleth (Ecclesiastes) underlines the same point. The Good News Bible catches the flavour of this message very well:

> Why do people commit crimes so readily? Because crime is not punished quickly enough. A sinner may commit a hundred crimes and still live. Oh yes I know what they say: 'If you obey God everything will be all right, but it will not go well for the wicked. Their life is like a shadow and they will die young because they do not obey God.' But this is nonsense. Look at what happens in the world; sometimes righteous men get the punishment of the wicked, and wicked men get the reward of the righteous. I say it is hebel.

From the following section we see Qoheleth's way of working. He was the one who sought wisdom. He tells us:

> When I set my mind to acquiring wisdom
> and to see the business that is done on earth,
> that one cannot see sleep by day or night;
> > Then I saw all God's work
> that one cannot find out the work that is done under the sun,

in that one labours to seek but does not discover it;
even though the wise man claims to know he cannot find it out.

For I pondered all this, testing it all,
that the righteous and the wise and their deeds are in God's hands;
whether it is love or hate one does not know.
Everything before them is vanity.
Since a single fate comes to all –
the righteous and the sinner, the good, the clean and unclean,
the one who sacrifices and the one who does not,
the moral and the immoral, the one who takes an oath
and the one who is afraid to do so.
This is an evil thing in all that is done under the sun,
that one fate comes to all;
and also human hearts are full of wickedness
and madness in their minds and afterward to the dead.
For whoever is chosen among all the living has hope;
for a live dog is better than a dead lion.
Because the living know they will die; but the dead know nothing,
and they have no more reward, since the memory of them is lost.
Their love, their hate, and their passion have already perished,
and they no longer have any share in what transpires on earth.
(8:16 - 9:6; J. L. Crenshaw's translation, Ecclesiastes, 153, 158)

The source of Qoheleth's anxiety was his inability to discover what God was doing at any given moment. He found himself before the silence of eternity. True to his training as a wise man, Qoheleth gathered all available information and examined it. He concluded that God is indifferent to goodness. The fate of good people rests in divine hands and no one knows whether God looks on humans with a smile or a frown.

To dramatise the point about divine indifference, Qoheleth focuses on the hour of death. At that time it makes no difference whether one has been good or not, the same fate falls on all of us. He lists the various groups, noting that they all go the same way.

Qoheleth's humour comes in when he says: 'a live dog is better than a dead lion'. (9. 4) A live person of a low social rank is better off than a dead greater one. Everything that distinguished people as individuals has now vanished - those who lived passionately are now not moved by anything.

Qoheleth was involved in a personal search for truth (e.g. 1:12, 1:17, 2:13 etc.) The fruits of his search are summed up in the refrain that runs throughout the book:

'Vanity of vanities,' says Qoheleth, 'vanity of vanities, all is vanity:
(1:1, 12:8)

The word translated as 'vanity' is hebel. It refers to something ethereal and unreal, and its literal meaning is 'vapour'. Michael V. Fox speaks of the metaphoric transfer from the word 'vapour' that helps us see the way Qoheleth uses the word. It can be used to denote ephemerality, vanity, nothingness, mystery, deceit and senseless nonsense (*A Time*, p. 28-29).

Frank Crusemann even suggests 'shit' as a translation of hebel (*Crisis of Wisdom*, p. 57).

John Cruickshank, a Camusien scholar, sees parallels between Ecclesiastes and Albert Camus (*Albert Camus*, p. 44, 46). Michael V. Fox acknowledges this and says that a modern translation of hebel could be 'absurd'. Camus says that 'what is absurd is the confrontation of the irrational with the wild longing for clarity whose call echoes in the human heart'. (Albert Camus, *Myth*, p. 16). In the play Caligula, Cherea sees events following their course until they founder in sheer lunacy. The fear in Caligula is not just the fear of death but the fear of the absurd meaning of the life that Caligula forces on his subjects:

'All I wish is to regain some peace of mind in a world that has regained a meaning. What spurs me on is not ambition but fear, my very reasonable fear of that inhuman vision in which my life means no more than a speck of dust.'
(Camus, *Caligula and Three Other Plays*, p. 22).

The notion of life meaning no more than a speck spoke to my feelings when I felt alone. I felt dirty. I didn't matter - my life was no more than a speck of insignificant dust.

L 'Etranger (The Stranger) was written four years after Caligula. Meursault is the hero (or anti-hero) of the novel, and his story is that his father deserted his mother when he was a small child. His mother, whom he has sent to an old folks' home, dies and he comes to her funeral. But he is unable to show or feel any emotions and cannot cry as he sits by the corpse all night. Camus described Meursault as someone who was at zero-point in his life. He can't tune into life or relate - all is absurd, out of sync. After the funeral, Meursault meets a girl named Maria by a swimming pool and he sleeps with her on the same night. When Maria asks him to marry her, he replies 'perhaps'. Meursault gives the people the answers he thinks they expect to keep them at bay and to help him avoid the despair within.

Later in the book, Meursault befriends a pimp named Raymond, who has been involved in a fight with some Arabs. Meursault takes Raymond's gun away so that he won't use it. However, Meursault himself is attacked later and he shoots one of the Arabs, not once but many times. In his account of the incident he tells us:

> *I was conscious only of the cymbals of the sun clashing on my skull, and, less distinctly, of the keen blade of light flashing up from the knife, scarring my eyelashes, and gouging into my eyeballs. Then everything began to reel before my eyes, a fiery gust came from the sea, while the sky cracked in two, from end to end, and a great sheet of flame poured down through the rift. Every nerve in my body was a steel spring, and my grip closed on the revolver.*
>
> (*The Stranger*, p. 75ff)

Meursault tells us of the sensation:

> *It was the same sort of heat as at my mother's funeral, and I had the same disagreeable sensations - especially in my forehead, where all the veins seemed to be bursting through the skin. I couldn't stand it any longer.*

What is happening here is nothing other than Meursault's grief at his mother's death coming to the fore. He identified with his mother. He did not weep but he did identify with her. Like her, he expects nothing from life and to save himself from despair, he feigns indifference to all that goes on.

What then of the violence he uses in killing his attacker? He tells us:

> *I knew I 'd shattered the balance of the day, the spacious calm of this beach on which I had been happy. But I fired four shots more into the inert body... And each successive shot was another loud, fateful rap on the door of my undoing.*
>
> (*The Stranger*, p. 76)

He is like the rebel whom Camus describes in the book of that title. He says of the rebel: 'He confronts an order of things which oppress him with an insistence on a kind of right not to be oppressed beyond the limit that he can tolerate.'

This same protest is the clue to another sudden explosion which Meursault experiences. This time it is with the prison chaplain who forces his way in to him and tries to force him to confess before his execution. Meursault is not indifferent to the guillotine, but he has schooled himself to appear to be so. When the priest asks him to call him 'Father' and insists that he is on Meursault's side and will pray for him even though his heart is hardened, something breaks in Meursault and he starts yelling at the priest, shouting insults at the top of his voice. It is here that we see the great hopelessness that gripped him and his mother before him. He is aware that he will die, and die alone. It is better to burn than to disappear, he tells the priest, challenging the latter's ordered universe with the vision of the absurd. The certainty of death makes it a matter of indifference to Meursault whether he has lived 'authentically' or 'inauthentically'. In an absurd world, 'nothing, nothing has the least importance and I know quite well why'.

He feels his approaching death, and looks with disdain at the ideas of solidarity that people have tried to foist on him in the years of his life:

What difference could they make to me, the deaths of others, or a mother's love, or his God; or the way a man decides to live, the fate he thinks he chooses, since one and the same fate was bound to 'choose' not only me but thousands of millions of privileged people who, like him, called themselves my brothers... All alike would be condemned to die one day... And what difference could it make if, after being charged with murder, he were executed because he didn't weep at his mother's funeral, since it all came to the same thing in the end?

(*The Stranger*, p. 182)

In the acceptance of his fate Meursault achieves a transformation and even a sort of peace.

Another artist of the absurd deserves a brief note here. Samuel Beckett belonged to the Theatre of the Absurd. When he was a young student he wandered through the poorer sections of Dublin, where he saw much poverty and misery. He felt he could no longer pledge allegiance to a God who would allow such suffering. Once, when he was interviewed about his play 'Waiting for Godot', and he was asked if the mysterious Mr. Godot was really God, Beckett responded that if he had meant God, he would have said God. But toward the end of his life, he said he wondered if he had really meant God after all. Beckett too was wrestling with what he saw of God's world and with God. Elie Wisel, in his disturbing work Night, describes how his faith in a great God evaporated in the concentration camp. The 'absurd' is a frightening view of the world. It is in the spirit of Ecclesiastes, (Qoholeth) and Psalm 73:2-14.

Before I move on to how the psalmist faced this tension in his life, I would just like to add the following note on Camus. When he wrote Sisyphus, Caligula and L'Etranger, Camus was fighting with deep hurt in his own life. His first marriage had failed. Later on he would write La Peste (The Plague), in which he placed individual responsibility at the feet of all public choices. He speaks of heroism and of ordinary people doing extraordinary things out of decency. He places these events in an allegorical story, set in Oran in North Africa where the bubonic plague strikes. Tarrou says:

> 'We are all in the plague...all I know is that one must do one's best not to be a plague victim...and that is why I have decided to reject everything that directly or indirectly, makes people die or justifies making them die.'
>
> (The Plague, p. 206)

This is the voice of Camus and it sketches out the position he would take towards ideology or anything that would kill innocent human beings, especially children. Camus was hitting out at dogmatic, intolerant people and the positions they adopted; at conformity, compliance and cowardice in all the public forms they manifest themselves. He used the allegory of the plague for this. At one stage he says in the book that the only answer to the plague is decency (p. 136). This statement is at once simple and yet wholly revolutionary. If, for instance, in the area of abuse, there was a sense of decency, then many would be spared innocent suffering and those who are injured might receive help. In so many areas (and here I think sadly of the church), this decency had been lacking.

Also in La Peste Dr. Rieux rebels against an order of creation or a God which causes an innocent child to suffer. What he hates is death and disease. Maurice Zundel was very moved by Camus. For Zundel God lives in the heart of each person and any offence against the person is also against God. To kill a human being is the same as killing God. Camus wrote a touching letter to Zundel to discuss his views on the sufferings of the innocent but before they could meet Camus was killed in a car accident (see Rouiller, *Le Scandale*, p. 17f). He moved from *L'Etranger* to more involvement in affirming humanity and individual human beings. Towards the end of his life Camus was working towards the idea of love as being the key to existence. He would say that there is tragedy in not loving and we are all dying of this tragedy, for violence and hate dry up the heart. (See Wink, p. 297; F. Chavanes, *Il Faut Vivre Maintenent*, p. 187-193). Tragically he lost his life in a car accident before this vision could come to full fruition.

Before I move on to see how the psalmist began to cope with the absurdity of existence, I wish to pause for a moment to remember the chilling end of *The Plague*:

> *And, indeed, as he listened to the cries of joy rising from the town, Rieux remembered that such joy is always imperilled. He knew what those jubilant crowds did not know but could have learned from books: that the plague bacillus never dies or disappears for good; that it can lie dormant for years and years in furniture and linen-chests; that it bides its time in bedrooms, cellars, trunks, and bookshelves; and that perhaps the day would come when, for the bane and the enlightening of men, it roused up its rats again and sent them forth to die in a happy city.*
>
> *(The Plague*, p. 252)

Life faces all of us with choices and if we lack a sense of decency and use people, then people will be hurt and destroyed. In his lifetime, Camus condemned fascism, the Gulags, Stalin's trials and totalitarianism wherever he found it. All these were manifestations of the plague. Camus centres his arguments on the dignity of each person, which is how he wrestled with the absurd.

Facing Life Anew

Qoheleth showed the limits of wisdom as he found it and he told us 'all is absurd (hebel) He did not himself know his time or place in the world, but by this diagnosis of life and its absurdity he enabled others to explore. Georges Bernanos once said, 'In order to be prepared to hope in what does not deceive, we must first lose hope in everything that deceives.' This is what Qoheleth helps us do. The psalmist in Psalm 73 had now seen the things that disappoint, so he seeks grounds for hope, a hope that does not deceive. He tells us:

> *If I had said, 'I will talk on in this way,'*
> *I would have been untrue to the circle of your children.*
> *But when I thought how to understand this,*
> *it seemed to me a wearisome task,*
> *until I went into the sanctuary of God:*
> *then I perceived their end.*
> *Truly you set them in slippery places:*
> *you make them fall to ruin.*
> *How they are destroyed in a moment,*
> *swept away utterly by terrors!*
> *They are like a dream when one awakes:*
> *on awaking you despise their phantoms.*
>
> (Ps 73:15-20)

He interrupts his account of the way he found things. If he had given way to his impulses of rebellion, anger and revenge he would have betrayed the circle of God's children. Now he sees the children of God as the pure in heart. I use this verse to think of the good and kind who really embody God's love in their hearts. I have met such people and they have affirmed my faith in humanity, a faith that was once broken and which, for a time, I believed could never be repaired.

The psalmist now strains his eyes to penetrate the darkness that hid God from him. He receives insight when he comes into the sanctuary of God, into God's presence. The man who is pure in heart, Martin Buber tells us, experiences that God is good to him. The temple can mean the sphere of God's holiness. Jesus reminds us we must worship in spirit and truth (Jn. 4:23).

For a time this access seemed blocked to me, but I could only pray in faith and darkness. Eventually the love of compassionate friends rekindled hope in me. They were the living expression of God's love.

The psalmist perceives the true end of the wicked. The wicked, Buber tells us, are those who are impure in heart. He tells us that in modern thought the wicked are as if they did not exist. In the end, they face the pain of their non-existence. Their life is set in 'slippery places'. They are like Dostoyevsky's character Stavrogin in *The Devils*. He does not love, only uses and abuses people. He believes himself fully autonomous with no need of God or human beings. Ultimately he destroys himself. He lived in a world without love, only abuse, where he neither gave nor received love. This destroyed love and this led to his end.

I feel the same way about these lines as I felt with Psalm 8 and other psalms of praise. I remember the years when I felt a non-person. My days were dark and tears and depression were my daily bread. My heart sank when I read these words about being in God's presence. Yet I continued to pray then almost as a protest against the darkness. It was hoping against hope. The opening lines of Psalm 63 were precious to me, too, in helping me to keep up hope:

> *O God, you are my God, I seek you*
> *my soul thirsts for you: my flesh faints for you,*
> *As in a dry weary land where there is no water.*
> (Ps 63:1)

Loving kindness (*hesed*) and peace (*shalom*) were things that were remote and I used these words to pray my need for kindness and peace.

When someone is healed others are drawn into the ambit of that healing. Simone Weil is one person who made the journey of which Psalm 73 speaks. She was a French philosopher who died during the Second World War. She worked in London for the French resistance, making herself eat only what those in occupied territories ate, which led to her death. I know that Camus was influenced by her writings but until I read a work by Howard Mumma, I had not realised that they were friends (see Mumma, *Albert Camus and the Minister*). Indeed, Mumma shows that, from his friendship with Weil, Camus was moving nearer to Christianity in his search for meaning and truth.

Simone was like the psalmist in our psalm. She spoke of 'affliction', although she would admit her experiences weren't pure affliction because she had the support of family and friends. She described affliction (malheur) in the following words:

> *Affliction causes God to be absent for a time, more absent than a*
> *dead man, more absent than light in the utter darkness of a cell. A*

kind of horror submerges the whole soul. During this absence there is nothing to love. What is terrible is that if, in this darkness where there is nothing to love, the soul ceases to love, God's absence becomes final. The soul has to go on loving in the void, or at least to go on wanting to love, though it may be only with an infinitesimal part of itself. Then, one day, God will come to show himself to this soul and to reveal the beauty of the world to it, as in the case of Job. But if the soul stops loving it falls, even in this life, into something which is almost equivalent to hell.

(Weil, *Science, Necessity of love of God*, p. 172)

In her later writings, *The Love of God and Affliction* and *Forms of the Implicit Love of God,* Weil reveals more of what affliction means. Affliction takes possession of the soul and brands it to the depths with the mark of a slave. It implies long and frequent physical pain. It implies social degradation. The one afflicted feels scorn, disgust, and self-loathing. Affliction leaves the victim writhing on the earth like a half-crushed worm.

The principal effect of affliction is the feeling that God is absent for a time, more absent than one who has died. A kind of horror overtakes the soul. The soul must go on loving and when it does it sees the presence of divine grace. If the soul can persevere in love, God does reveal himself. Now we rejoin Simone in her journey to meet God.

She experienced something of this pain when she gave up her work of teaching and went to work as a labourer in a factory. She did not see grace at work there. What she did see was the extreme degree to which human beings could be dominated, body and soul, without having it in their power to escape domination. Many who find themselves in abusive situations can relate to this. Simone described in a little passage what she felt like after months of degradation. She has just been to the dentist:

Upon leaving the dentist's...and in getting on the W-bus, a bizarre reaction. How is it that I, the slave, can get on the bus and ride it for 12 sous just like anybody else? What an extraordinary favour! If someone brutally forced me to get off, saying that these convenient means of transportation were not for me, that I could only walk, I believe that would have seemed entirely natural to me. Slavery has made me lose all sense of having rights.

(See Springsted, *Suffering of Love*, p. 26)

One can learn to think of affliction as a way of life. One can look in wonder at someone who is kind, wondering how they could bother with one who is worthless. Harshness, cruelty and harsh words are all that one in this condition of a slave believes they are worth. This takes me back to the days of my deepest loneliness.

After Simone left the factory, she went through a time of great despondency. She felt helpless in the face of the affliction of others. She saw Charlie Chaplin's film *Modern Times* and came to appreciate the scene in which Chaplin is sucked into the machine.

God did come to Simone and led her to a new way of life. The first experience she had was when she was on holiday in Portugal in a little fishing village. One evening there was a candle-lit procession in honour of a local saint. While watching the faces of the people, Simone perceived something poignant and beautiful. She said she realised that Christianity is the religion of 'slaves' (so she called those who suffered affliction): 'Slaves cannot help belonging to it and I among others.' (*Waiting for God*, p. 68) Simone saw that in Christ, God crosses the void between heaven and earth and comes to us in our affliction and shares it with us.

A further deepening of Simone's journey to God happened when she visited the monastery of Solesmes for the Easter ceremonies. Here she met a young Englishman who introduced her to the English metaphysical poets. Among these was George Herbert, whose poem 'Love' runs as follows:

> *Love bade me welcome; yet my soul drew back,*
> *Guilty of dust and sinne,*
> *But quick-ey 'd Love, observing me grow slack*
> *From my first entrance in,*
> *Drew nearer to me, sweetly questioning*
> *If I lack'd any thing.*
>
> *'A guest,' I answer 'd, 'worthy to be here':*
> *Love said, 'You shall be he.'*
> *I the unkind, ungrateful? Ah my dear,*
> *I cannot look on thee.'*
>
> *Love took my hand, and smiling did reply,*
> *'Who made the eyes but I?'*

'Truth Lord, but I have marr 'd them, let my shame
Go where it doth deserve.'
'And know you not,' says Love, 'who bore the blame?'
'My dear, then I will serve.'
'You must sit down, sayes Love, and taste my meat.'
So I did sit and eat.

As with the Gregorian plain chant at Solesmes, Simone was at first conscious of the authentic quality of Herbert's work: 'I used to think that I was merely saying beautiful verse, but though I did not know it, the recitation had the effect of a prayer. And it happened that as I was saying this poem... Christ himself came down and he took me.' In the stillness of the senses, the imagination mute while her body suffered - she was victim of violent migraine attacks at this time - Simone was brought into 'the presence of a love similar to the one expressed in the smile on the face of the beloved'. (See Cabaud, *Simone Weil*, p. 170).

She felt herself enveloped by love and she sought others to share the love she felt. She lived out Psalm 73 in her person. Simone is the honorary patron saint of outsiders. She sought out the broken, the afflicted and tried to ease their pain by giving of herself and her love. The love Jesus shared when 'afflicted' is the paradigm for all love. Simone saw Christ in all the afflicted and she was like him in giving of herself. Her experience of love was not just for herself. By sharing her experience she allowed others to come to that same love. In the same way as George Herbert's poem became a prayer for Simone, I pray that Psalm 73 might be similar for those who suffer 'affliction' and through the words of the psalm they may come to know the presence of love.

Taking Wrong directions on the Road back Home

The next two lines of Psalm 73 speak directly to my heart:

When my soul was embittered,
When I was pricked in heart,
I was stupid and ignorant;
I was like a brute beast toward you.
(Ps.73:21-22)

When my soul was embittered I was full of anger, resentment and negative feelings towards the world and everyone in it. I discovered depths of anger in myself that shocked me and I felt even more lost. Much as I tried to bury my anger, it often surfaced unexpectedly. The psalms helped me come to a safer place where I could acknowledge negative feelings and reach understanding.

The so-called cursing and imprecation psalms are something that are kept discreetly from view. In Psalm 58 the psalmist prays in the following way:

O God, break the teeth in their mouths;
tear out the fangs of the young lions, O LORD!
Let them vanish like water that runs away:
like grass let them be trodden down and wither.

Let them be like the snail that dissolves into slime;
like the untimely birth that never sees the sun.
Sooner than your pots can feel the heat of thorns,
whether green or ablaze, may he sweep them away!
(Ps.58: 6-9)

Praying to God to break the teeth of those who hurt us seems strange to many of us. Psalm 109 has the same note as this. Here the psalmist prays in the following way for the wicked one he despises:

When he is tried, let him be found guilty;
let his prayer be counted as sin.
May his days be few;
may another seize his position.
May his children be orphans,
and his wife a widow.
May his children wander about and beg;
may they be driven out of the ruins they inhabit.
May the creditor seize all that he has;
may strangers plunder the fruits of his toil.
May there be no one to do him a kindness,
nor anyone to pity his orphaned children.
May his posterity be cut off;
may his name be blotted out in

the second generation.
May the iniquity of his father
be remembered before the LORD.
and do not let the sin of his
mother be blotted out.

(Ps.109:7-14)

Psalm 137 was made very popular by the group Boney M, who recorded a single entitled 'By the Rivers of Babylon'. It speaks of the episode where the captors ask the Israelites to sing one of Zion's songs. Yet in this version and also in such places as the Liturgy of the Hours the final verse is kept directly out of sight. It reads:

O daughter Babylon, you devastator!
Happy shall they be who pay you back
what you have done to us!
Happy shall they be who take your little ones
and dash them against the rock!

(Ps 137:8-9)

These three psalms show that the psalmist is brutally honest about what some of us would have called 'unworthy feelings'. He brings his anger and desire for vengeance before God's loving kindness, acknowledging the reality of vengeful feelings in us. These psalms speak about the unfairness and exploitation that evoke rage. There is an act of faith by which we can approach the presence of God whose rule is marked by faithfulness and compassion. Such rage is not only brought into Yahweh s presence, it is submitted to him and relinquished to him. Yahweh is one who takes seriously the well-being of his people. The raw speech of rage can be submitted to Yahweh because He will listen and act (Brueggemann, *Message of the Psalms*, p. 85) It is a safe place to own our emotions, negative as they may be and, in the light of acceptance, accept ourselves and in God's grace find constructive ways of dealing with anger. In union with God, anger can become a vehicle for change.

In the days of my affliction I had no way of coping with the anger and this only added to my deep depression. Coming in faith to the psalms helps me acknowledge my emotions and seek ways of expressing my emotions in constructive ways. Anger at injustice can be a share in God's anger at the treatment of his beloved.

In coming to know God, the psalmist need no longer be like the wild-beast.

Nevertheless I am continually
with you;
you hold me ? my right hand.
You guide me with your counsel,
and afterward you will receive me with honour.'
Whom have I in heaven but you?
And there is nothing on earth
that I desire other than you.
My flesh and my heart may fail,
but God is the strength of my
heart and my portion forever.

(Ps 73:23-26)

Now the psalmist is with God who guides him and gives him counsel. The line afterwards 'you will receive me with honour' does not, according to Buber, yet refer to immortality of the soul (*The Heart Determines*, p. 207), but it does reflect the seed of an idea that will come to realisation in the resurrection of Christ from the dead.

Simone Weil, who had studied classical Greek Tragedy, saw intimations of Jesus in these dramas (Weil, *Intimations*, p. 188). All the violence of the tragedy finishes with the death of the hero, who somehow saves the people. In Jesus, Simone saw that all the hatred, rejection and affliction visited on him ended with his death, but with his rising from the dead and forgiving those who crucified him, he now allows us to share in his life-giving spirit. The words of the psalm take on a new life in the one who cries to Jesus. One can say with him 'God is the strength of my heart and my potion forever.' Psalm 73 ends with the following refrain, which repeats themes we have come across in the past:

Indeed, those who are far from you will perish;
you put an end to those who are false to you.
But for me it is good to be near God:
I have made the Lord GOD my refuge,
to tell of all your works.

(Ps.73:27-28)

I leave the final word with Reinhold Schneider, a dramatist who suffered much from depression. He finds that he is not alone in his suffering, something we saw in Psalm 73. He says:

'Shudder no longer before what is extraordinary
And look piously at the ultimate cruelties:
God suffers with you, you disappear into him.'
(see Von Balthasar, *Tragedy Under Grace*, p. 205)

Chapter 7

A Cry of Need and Hope

Throughout these meditations I have shared my battle with the false images of God that come across my path. It was a world filled with anxiety and little love. It also felt like a world where I could not speak of my pain and loneliness, but grief would not be silent. Philip Larkin expressed similar feelings in his poem 'If grief could burn out':

If grief could burn out
Like a sunken coal,
The heart would rest quiet,
The unrent soul
Be still as a veil;
But I have watched all night.

The fire grow silent,
The grey ash soft:
And I stir the stubborn flint
The flames have left,
And grief stirs, and the deft
Heart lies impotent.

I often wished that grief would just disappear or burn out and leave me alone, but like the poet, I find that grief stirs and leaves the heart impotent.

Yet the psalmists and Jesus shared another God who is big enough to hear my confused pleas and hurt feelings. Jesus spoke of the need of becoming like little children (Mk 10:13-24 etc.) Becoming like a little child and praying to God as I am is something that suddenly made sense to me when I discovered the following little story from Henri Nouwen:

John Fraser, the European correspondent of the Globe and Mail, one of Canada's national newspapers, came to visit Madame Vanier. I was invited for tea. We talked about the people of China, Tibet and the Dalai Lama, the Catholic Church in the Philippines and North Korea, and the Pope's recent visit to Holland. John Fraser is a well-travelled, very knowledgeable journalist who is both a keen observer of world events and a man with a deep personal interest in the religious life.

Among all his stories about world events, John told us a small story about his daughter Jessie. It is this story I will remember most:

'*One morning when Jessie was four years old, she found a dead sparrow in front of the living-room window. The little bird had killed itself by flying into the glass. When Jessie saw the dead bird she was both deeply disturbed and very intrigued. She asked me, "Where is the bird now?" I said I didn't know.*

"*Why did it die?*" *she asked.*

"*Well,*" *I said hesitantly, "because all birds return to the earth.*"

"*Oh,*" *said Jessie, "then we have to bury it.*"

A box was found, the little bird was laid in the box, a paper napkin was added as a shroud, and a few minutes later a little procession was formed with Daddy, Mama, Jessie, and her little sister. I carried the box, Jessie the homemade cross. After a grave was dug and the little sparrow was buried, I put a piece of moss over the grave and Jessie planted the cross upon it. Then I asked Jessie, "Do you want to say a prayer?"

"*Yes,*" *replied Jessie firmly, and after having told her baby sister in no uncertain terms to fold her hands, she prayed: "Dear God, we have buried this little sparrow. Now you be good to her or I will kill you. Amen.*"

As we walked home, I said to Jessie, "You didn't have to threaten God."

Jessie answered, "I just wanted to be sure."
(*The Road to Daybreak*, p. 167)

Little Jessie spoke to God in a way that shocked her father, as it would most of us brought up in a certain way. She trusted God to be big enough to handle anything she said and what she said, she said firmly.

I remember another incident from the cartoon show 'The Simpsons'. Ned Flanders, the Simpsons' next-door neighbour, has just lost his wife and he is angry with God. He refuses to go to church one Sunday, to the shock and horror of his two sons. The next scene shows Ned driving feverishly towards the church, looking up to heaven and saying, 'Sorry,

God, I'm sorry.' I more often feel like Ned than like little Jessie. I'm full of fear before God that he is not big enough to accept me and my feelings. Yet when I pray and meditate on the psalms, as I have done in this little work, I consciously leave this world of fear and dare to take the chance that God is big enough to hear, accept and heal me.

For a while, when I was engulfed in loneliness and confusion, I tried to avoid coming to this decision. I preferred to flee God in my own heart. Francis Thompson, the poet, expressed this plight:

> *I fled Him, down the nights and down the days;*
> *I fled Him, down the arches of the years;*
> *I fled Him, down the labyrinthine ways*
> *Of my own mind; and in the mist of tears*
> *I hid from Him, and under running laughter.*
> *Up vistaed hopes I sped;*
> *And shot, precipitated,*
> *Adown Titanic glooms of chasmed fears,*
> *From those strong feet that followed, followed after.*
> *But with unhurrying chase,*
> *And unperturbed pace,*
> *Deliberate speed, majestic instancy,*
> *They beat - and a Voice beat*
> *More instant than the Feet -*
> *'All things betray thee, who betrayest Me.*
> <div align="right">(<i>'The Hound of Heaven'</i>)</div>

I too felt like fleeing God 'down the labyrinthine ways of my own mind, adown Titanic glooms of chasmed fears'. It was no good. I had to come back to start all over again. I felt as one whose whole world has been destroyed and he must try and rebuild it, brick by brick. What I have shared in these reflections is my journey of rebuilding, relating again to God and others in the face of depression, despair and anxiety. I share so that others may know they are not alone. I remember a young lady who came to me on my journey through loneliness. She had been abused and she decided to trust me with her story. I was able to be with her and explain something of my own story. As time passed, she began to heal and her confidence was restored. I felt I was in that strange place where a student overtakes his teacher. At a certain stage, some of their better students surpass them, understanding more than their former masters. This is what happened to me. Vicky (not her real name) became more confident than I had ever been and much more outgoing. I was no longer the healer but the one who was being ministered to. The healed had become the healer.

The Two Poles of Prayer

In the meditations and prayers I have shared with you, there are two poles. The first pole is myself and how I feel and the second pole is God's response to my plight. There is a little book I found, called Healing of Soul, Healing of Body. Some of the psalms it uses helped me see the first pole out of which I operated. They helped me face the fact that, even though I lived in much fear, I was not alone. Rabbi Harlen J. Wechsler offers the following as his translation and interpretation of Psalm 16:

> *These are among David's golden words:*
> *'Watch over me, God,*
> *for I seek refuge in You.*
> *You said to the Lord:*
> *'You are my Master,*
> *but my good fortune is not Your concern.*
> *'Rather, the holy ones on the earth*
> *- You care for them*
> *and for the great ones whom I should emulate.*
> *'When their pain multiplies,*
> *they know to speedily turn to another.*
> *But I cannot even pour their libations because of guilt,*
> *I cannot even lift their names to my lips.'*

Those lines help me see the inadequacy, distance and unworthiness I often felt. I sometimes thought that my pain was not God's concern. His concern was only for the lucky and the few, but not me.

From verse 7, the psalmist sees that these thoughts are just feelings and lack no substance. He intuits that God doesn't want him to wallow in sorrow. The next verses constitute an act of faith, where the psalmist reaches out to God in the face of his despair:

> *I will bless the Lord who counsels me,*
> *though at night my conscience afflicts me.*
> *1 keep the Lord continually before me;*

because of God-Who-is-my-Right-Hand,
I shall not break down.
So my mind is happy,
my whole being joyful;
even my body rests secure.
For You shall not abandon my soul
to the world of the dead,
nor let the one who loves You
see his own grave.
Give me directions on life's road.
With Your Presence,
I am filled up with joys,
with the delights that ever come
from Your Strong Arm.

There is always the act of faith in the psalms that even when we express our fears, limits and confused feelings, God is present there and accepts us and loves us.

Rabbi Harold M. Schulweiss, in his meditation based on Psalm 77, offers the following verses as his meditation on Psalm 77. He begins:

When I cry my voice trembles with fear
When I call out it cracks with anger.
How can I greet the dawn with song
when darkness eclipses the rising sun

To whom shall I turn
when the clouds of the present eclipse the rays of tomorrow

Turn me around to yesterday
that I may be consoled by its memories.

It is a prayer offered when he trembles with fear and anger. The brightness of the dawn is darkened by the sufferings of the prayer. He wonders where can he rum in his hour of need. Then he comes to seek the presence of God. Finally he remembers the great acts of God for those whom He loves:

Were not the seas split asunder
did we not once walk together through the waters
to the dry side

Did we not bless the
bread that came forth from the heavens

Did your voice not reach my ears
and direct my wanderings

The waters, the lightning, the thunder
remind me of yesterday's triumphs?

Let the past offer proof of tomorrow
let it be my comforter and guarantor.

The memories of God's people reveal His love and care for them. For me this love is revealed in the person of Jesus, who especially treasured those who were broken and lost.

The poem ends with the following lines:

I have been here before
known the fright and found your companionship.
I enter the sanctuary again
to await the echo of your promise.

These lines help me remember the times I turned to God and found solace there. When I pray the psalms I enter God's presence again, his sanctuary, to 'await the echo of his promise.' I await the echo of his voice, his word of compassion and healing.

Here the emphasis falls on the first pole of my prayer. The other pole is God's response. I find the echo of His promise is His Word made flesh, Jesus the Christ. To begin to hear what God has to say in Jesus is an enormous task and way beyond the scope of this present work. Here I will dwell on one aspect of Jesus - his mission as suffering servant. Again I have to return to the Hebrew Bible to know Jesus 'from the inside' (Buber). Between myself and God I often placed the fake picture of God. In Jesus, I allow God to speak as he is. Deuteuro-Isaiah (Is 40-55) was written during the exile (582 B.C.) It follows on the work of Jeremiah, who had complained that he was lonely because of God's word (Jer. 15-7). He helped the people face the pain of a failed world. He paved the way for Deuteuro-Isaiah who could come and speak God's word of consolation and comfort for His people (see Is 40:1). By embracing the pain helped by Jeremiah, the time was now ripe when a new orientation was possible for the people (Deutero-Isaiah). Both Jeremiah and the unknown prophet of Deutero-Isaiah were poets who subverted the old ways of looking at things and created the possibility for a new understanding of God. Poets and artists are the people who can inflame the hearts of the people with hope and for that very reason they are often under suspicion in totalitarian regimes.

My particular interest is the figure of the suffering servant who appears in 52:13 - 53:12. This is the faith of the so-called servant songs, the others being 42:1-9,49:1-7 and 50:4-9. These works are poems and by their nature, they refuse to be precise or to give information. They are evocative and can refer to the people or to a particular individual who represents the people. Martin Buber, in his work *The Prophetic Faith*, argues that throughout history there appear people who embrace the vocation spoken about in this poem. One man he had in mind was his friend Franz Rosenweig, who was very ill towards the end of his life, though he still collaborated with Buber in the German translation of the Hebrew Bible. While he suffered, those around him found themselves enriched by his presence. For me as a Christian, Jesus embodies the suffering servant vocation in a radical way, as the Son of God. The poem of the suffering servant begins:

See, my servant shall prosper;
he shall be exalted and lifted up,
and shall be very high.
(Is 52:13)

For this section I use Walter Brueggemann's translation of the suffering-servant poem (see Is 40-66, p. 141-150). The opening line voices the ultimate resolve of Yahweh that the servant (whoever he may be) will in the end be honoured and exalted. The opening verse is matched by the concluding assertion about the exultation of the servant (53:10-12).

Just as there were many who were astonished at him –
so marred was his appearance, beyond human semblance,

and his form beyond that of mortals –
so he shall startle many nations;
kings shall shut their mouths because of him; for that which had
not been told them they shall see, and that which they had not
heard they shall contemplate.

(52:14-15)

Verse 14 portrays the servant as a marked, distorted figure. He is not one of the beautiful people. He is rather a disfigured person upon whom one can hardly bear to look. This sorry portrayal is abruptly countered in verse 15 by the assertion that nations and kings are awed by the servant and assume a respectful silence before this mysterious one. The humiliated one becomes the exalted one in whom Yahweh works.

The poem must be understood in the context of the Isaiah tradition. Therefore as the servant is Israel (a common assumption of Jewish interpretation) we see that the theme of humiliation and exaltation serves the Isaiah rendering of Israel, for Israel in tradition is the humiliated (exalted) people of Israel, who by the powerful intervention of Yahweh is about to become the exalted restored people of Zion. This drama of Israel is the first subject of the poetry. As a Christian I see the servant relived in the figure of Jesus in a unique way. He is the very son of God. In the passage from St. Paul, Philippians 2:5-11, it says of Jesus:

Who, though he was in the form of God.
did not regard equality with God
as something to be exploited,
but emptied himself,
taking the form of a slave,
being born in human likeness.
And being found in human form,
he humbled himself
and became obedient to the point of death –
even death on a cross.

Therefore God also highly
exalted him
and gave him the name
that is above every name,
so that at the name of Jesus

every knee should bend,
in heaven and on earth and
under the earth,
and every tongue should confess
that Jesus Christ is Lord,
to the glory of God the Father.
(Phil 2:6-11)

Here we see the theme of humiliation in the death of Jesus and the theme of exaltation as God raises him from the dead. The poem of the suffering servant is important for understanding Jesus is also in Acts 9, where Philip interprets this part of Isaiah as referring to Jesus.

Walter Brueggemann reminds us that the Jewish conviction of Israel going from exilic humiliation to restored exaltation and the Christian conviction of Jesus being humiliated in crucifixion and exalted at Easter have for a long time been in deep tension. Brueggemann's own judgement is that it is more important to recognise the communality and parallel structure of Jewish and Christian claims at the core of faith (p. 143). Isaiah 52:13 - 52:12 is a poem and does not permit one single solution. Rilke speaks of someone reading a poem and realising many more meanings than the poet intended. Here there is room for both interpretations and, following Buber's lead, we can see the poem realised in the hearts of others too, in the cause of history. The example of Franz Rosenweig in his last years once again comes to mind. For me as a Christian the realisation of the suffering servant vocation in Jesus is important. As son of God he lived this in a special way.

Who has believed what we have heard?
And to whom has the arm of the LORD been revealed?
(53:1)

This passage bears witness not only to the power of Yahweh and the destiny of the servant, but also to the faith of the community that experiences healing from the suffering one.

For he grew up before him like a young plant, and like a root
out of dry ground; he had no form or majesty that we should look at
him, nothing in his appearance that we should desire him. He was
despised and rejected by others; a man of suffering and acquainted

with infirmity; and as one from whom others hide their faces he was
despised, and we held him of no account.

(53:2-3)

The servant was a rejected person, perhaps ostracised, perhaps disabled, of whom nothing was expected. He was not one of the great ones on the earth:

Surely he has borne our infirmities
and carried our diseases;
yet we accounted him stricken,
struck down by God, and afflicted.
But he was wounded for our transgressions,
crushed for our iniquities;
upon him was the punishment that made us whole,
and by his bruises we are healed.
All we like sheep have gone astray;
we have all turned to our own way,
and the LORD had laid on him the iniquity of us all.

(vv. 4-6)

This very one took on himself disabilities and diseases, all caused by sin. By accepting all this, the servant was crushed, wounded and broken. Yet we are the ones who are healed. In Isaiah 63:9 we have the line speaking of Yahweh: 'In all our afflictions he was afflicted.' All our sufferings are God's and we see this in Jesus in a special way who took on himself the wounds of sin and disease to the point of his breakdown and death. The servant is one who is in sympathy with Yahweh, and who has compassion for the people. By acting the role of servant he brings healing to a broken relationship. In the poem on the work of the servant we find a section that is dominated by first person-pronouns: 'me, our, us etc.' This is not a cold detached statement. It is rather our voice of hope, poured out in passionate, personal terms.

He was oppressed, and he was afflicted,
yet he did not open his mouth;
like a lamb that is led to the slaughter,
and like a sheep that before its shearers is silent,
so he did not open his mouth.

By a perversion of justice he was taken away.
Who could have imagined his future?
For he was cut off from the land of the living,
stricken for the transgression of my people.
They made his grave with the wicked
and his tomb with the rich,
although he had done no violence,
and there was no deceit in his mouth.

(53:7-9)

The servant was oppressed, afflicted and done in by a 'perversion of justice'. He was not guilty and thus should have received no punishment. He is the righteous sufferer we have met in the psalms and in Job. In the Gospel of John Jesus is referred to as 'the lamb of God who takes away the sin of the world' (Jn. 1:29). His is a life given for others - no satisfaction of anger, a giving of oneself to the point of death. He did this so we could realise that all pain and rejection die with him and when he rises again he gives us new life. My sufferings are his. I am on a journey from Gethsemane to Calvary to Easter day with Jesus. This is something Paul describes in Philippians 3:7-11:

Yet whatever gains I had, these I have come to regard
as loss because of Christ.
More than that, I regard everything as loss because
of the surpassing value of knowing Christ Jesus my
Lord. For his sake I have suffered the loss of all
things, and I regard them as rubbish, in order that I
may gain Christ.
and be found in him. not having a righteousness of my
own that comes from the law, but one that comes
through faith.
I want to know Christ and the power of his
resurrection and the sharing of his sufferings by
becoming like him in his death.
if somehow I may attain the resurrection from the dead.

F.F. Bruce says that Paul's knowledge of Jesus is personal knowledge. It includes the experience of being loved by him and loving Jesus and those whom he loves in return (Phil 1:13). Paul is on a pilgrimage with Jesus until he comes to new life in him.

In the second letter to the Corinthians, Paul speaks of his personal experience of suffering, including a near-death experience (2 Cor. 1:10, 8-10). He points out to the audience that even though he suffered much in his following of Jesus, 'in us, then, death is at work; in you life'. (2 Cor. 3:12). This is Paul's living out of the suffering servant's vocation in following Jesus. Death is at work in him but God works through this to bring life to others. God's presence is evident in those who suffer. He chooses to reveal his love through the suffering servant.

The final section of the suffering-servant poem reads:

Yet it was the will of the LORD to crush him with pain.
When you make his life an offering for sin,
he shall see his offspring, and shall prolong his days;
through him the will of the LORD shall prosper.
Out of his anguish he shall see light;
he shall find satisfaction through his knowledge,
the righteous one, my servant, shall make many righteous,
and he shall bear their iniquities.
Therefore I will allot him a portion with the great,
and he shall divide the spoil with the strong;
because he poured out himself to death,
and was numbered with the transgressors;
yet he bore the sin of many,
and made intercession for the transgressors.

(vv. 10-12.)

In verse 9 we seemed to have arrived at the end of the poem, yet it continues with the phrase 'Yet Yahweh' (v. 10). It is Yahweh, God, who insists the poem continues. The servant gave all and our God makes him receive all.

In verses 11b-12 the words are on the lips of Yahweh. The servant makes righteous those who are judged. Therefore God exalts the servant. The servant is one who stood in the midst of the afflicted and the sinful and now he is exalted. Some think the poem speaks of the resurrection. However this is not said, rather it is said that Yahweh exalts the servant. However, it certainly prepares the ground for the resurrection to take root in the hearts of the people. His life is fulfilled in the resurrection of Jesus from the dead. Jesus in his mission as a suffering servant shows us the depths to which God will go so that we may know we are loved and beloved of him.

There are others who, in their following of Jesus, have entered the suffering-servant vocation. I think of such people as Thérèse of Lisieux, Marthe Robin and Gemma Galgani. Though death and suffering were at work in them, in those who came into contact with them, life was at work. How many people discovered in the life of Thérèse a sister who radiated in her sufferings the love of
God to them?

I see Gerald Manley Hopkins, too, as having a share in the suffering-servant vocation. He was terribly depressed during the time he taught in Dublin. One of the 'terrible sonnets', 'Carrion Comfort', expresses Hopkins' state as the end of his life approached:

NOT, I'll not, carrion comfort, Despair, not feast on thee;
Not untwist - slack they may be - these last strands of man
In me or, most weary, cry I can no more. I can;
Can something, hope, wish day come, not choose not to be.

But ah, but O thou terrible, why wouldst thou rude on me
Thy wring-world right foot rock? lay a lionlimb against me:
scan
With darksome devouring eyes my bruised bones? and fan,
O in turns of tempest, me heaped there; me frantic to avoid
thee and flee?

Still his basic vision was in Christ, what he called a 'Christed' vision. All the time, Hopkins looked to the comfort of the resurrection. In his 1888 poem *'That Nature is a Heraclitean Fine and of the Comfort of the Resurrection'*, he wrote at the end:

But vastness blurs and times beats level. Enough! the
Resurrection,
A heart's-clarion! Away grief's gasping, joyless days,
dejection.
Across my foundering deck shone
A beacon, an eternal beam. Flesh fade, and mortal trash
Fall to the residuary worm; world's wildfire, leave but ash:
In a flash, at a trumpet crash,
I am all at once what Christ is, since he was what I am, and
This Jack, joke, poor potsherd, patch, matchwood,

immortal diamond,
Is immortal diamond.

Through his sufferings, Hopkins is still called to new life. He saw his poetry as a form of sacrament. Through it the reader could be led from the darkness of despair to the brightness of new life.

He, Hopkins, was the suffering servant who shared the way in his poetry. God is present in all those who share in the suffering-servant vocation. This then shows us the sacrifice of love that they are prepared to make so that we may know we are loved. What can be said of all the wounded healers, the suffering servants, can be said of Jesus in a pre-eminent way: 'By his wounds we are healed.'

The place of the cross is vital for me in seeing God's love revealed in Jesus. Reading Paul Tillich was important for me in this regard. The cross is the ultimate or definitive revelation of God's love. Here there is no greater love than Jesus laying down his life for his friends. Jurgen Moltmann says that God is not more glorious than in Jesus' total giving of himself (*Crucified God*, p. 204). On the cross Jesus participates in our estrangement and alienation, suffering and death. It is here that God had chosen to be with us in Jesus. He had brought that separation and alienation to an end by entering into it.

Jesus works and implicates God his Father in all that he does. In the cross God takes the estrangement, the meaninglessness, and the despair of human existence into himself and they are stripped of their power to destroy. For me, this shows that my pain and false pictures of God are not the final reality. It is God's love that I look towards. Looking unto Jesus leads me from the false picture of God that abuse and rejection placed before me. I may not yet realise this fully but the cross remains a visible symbol for me of the way I must take. Tillich finds that here God manifests his power in weakness. God's activity 'must be understood as his participation in our estrangement and in its destructive consequences.' (*Systematic Theology*, Vol.11, p. 174)

God's participation in the negativity of existence is His expression of acceptance and love. Acceptance is an important word for Tillich (see *The Courage To Be*). Here it means an act by which God unites us with himself. Our loneliness, isolation and negative feelings about ourselves point us to the fact that we are in need of this loving union (*Systematic Theology*, Vol.111, p. 225). This acceptance is God's reconciling act and all that would hold us from God loses all its power. God's acceptance towards us is at the heights and depths of our human condition, because in Jesus he had participated in the negativities and contradictions that constitute our human existence. God's acceptance is not some kind of bland tolerance. On the cross he forgives and claims us.

Not to accept someone is tantamount to killing them. Abuse is an extreme form of this rejection. To live a life with God means having the courage to accept acceptance. It involves saying yes to life and, in the face of all the negative feelings, accepting the fact that before God we are accepted. Those who have been plunged into the deepest darkness know how difficult this is. The psalms I have meditated on and prayed enable us to acknowledge where we are coming from. We reach out in hope that the one who is love (1 Jn. 4:8, 16) will meet us in his Spirit and teach us in our hearts the love he revealed on the cross. 'Only by taking suffering and death upon himself could Jesus be the Christ, because only in this way could he participate in existence and conquer every force of estrangement which tried to dissolve his unity with God.' (Systematic Theology, Vol.11, p. 123). Only the man on the cross is the restoration in history of the eternal message that nothing can separate us from the love of God (see Rom 8: 35-39).

I have had this thought before when meditating on the cross. Living in a world of fear for so long made me feel that this love was not for me. Yet the cross is real and does not allow me to remain in fear. It is a visible expression of God saying to us all individually: 'I love you.' My own love is imperfect and I can impose my own lack of love unto God and create Him in the image of my own unloving. Jesus' total self-giving points me to the fact that this God I create is an idol and I must come anew to the presence of the living God with Jesus in the Spirit.

This journey to God is one that those who are afflicted with sorrow, distress, fear and loneliness long to embark on. The prayer-book of Jesus and Mary is the vehicle I have chosen to use in the work to share my journey in this regard. I do this, as I have said so often, so that those who weep and those who weep with those who weep may find the courage to hear that they are not alone and can reach out again, to the one who cares and loves. I also pray the words for them who fear and weep and cannot as yet make that journey. I make an act of faith that the God who revealed his love in Jesus is present in my words and accepts me where I am.

Postscript

The book, *The Song of Songs*, in the Old Testament is a collection of love-poetry written by lovers in love. Many writers, such as Rabbi Akiba, Origen and others, saw in those love songs an allegory of God's love for his people. Bernard of Clairvaux wrote 72 sermons on the first two chapters of The Song of Songs. Basically, the book is love poetry. In the evocative style of poetry the reader can see more meanings than the original writer intended. For me this means that reading The Song of Songs as love poetry and as an allegory are both possible. One doesn't exclude the other. In the Epilogue of the poem we are told that love is 'a flame of Yahweh himself. There is one poem that speaks gently. It is where the lover comes to the beloved and calls her gently to come to himself. It is for me the gentle call of God to the broken.

I leave you with the prayer and pray that you hear this voice.

My love lifts up his voice,
he says to me,
'Come then, my beloved,
my lovely one, come.
For see, winter, is past,
the rains are over and gone.
'Flowers are appearing on the earth.
The season of glad songs has come,
the cooing of the turtledove is heard in our land.
The fig tree is forming its first figs
and the blossoming vines give out their fragrance.
Come then, my beloved,
my lovely one, come.'   (Song 2: 10-13)

Bibliography

Anderson, B W, *Out of the Depths: The Psalms Speak for us Today* (Philadelphia, Westminster Press, 1983)

Auden, W H, *Collected Poems* (New York) Vintage Books, 1991

Balentine, Samuel E, *Prayer in the Hebrew Bible: The Drama of Divine-Human Dialogue* (OBT, Minneapolis, Fortress Press, 1993)

Bellow, Saul, *More Die of Heartbreak* (London, Penguin, 1996)

Bernanos, G, *The Diary of a Country Priest* (New York/London, Macmillan, 1937)

Bonhoeffer, D, *Prayerbook of the Bible* (Minneapolis, Fortress Press, 1996)

Booth, Wayne, *A Rhetoric of Irony* (Chicago University Press, 1974)

Bright, John, *'Jeremiah's Complaints: Liturgy or Expression of Personal Distress'* in Proclamation and Presence (Eds. John J Durham and JR Porter,   London, SCM Press, 1970)

Bruce, FF, *Philippians* (Peabody, MA, Hendrickson, 1989)

Brueggemann, Walter, *The Message of the Psalms* (Minneapolis, Augsburg, 1984)
'From Hurt to Joy, From Death to Life' in *The Psalms and the Life of Faith* (Minneapolis, Augsburg Fortress, 1995)
'The Formfulness of Grief in *The Psalms and the Life of Faith* (Minneapolis, Augsburg Fortress, 1995)
Isaiah 40-66 (Louisville, Westminster Press, 1998)
A Shape for Old Testament Theology I -Structure Legetimation - *Catholic Biblical Quarterly* -47 (1985) 28-46
A Shape for Old Testament Theology II - Embrace of Pain- *Catholic Biblical Quarterly* -47 (1985) 395-415
'Hopeful Imagination' (Philadelphia Fortress Press 1986)

Buber, Martin, *I and Thou* (New York, Scribner's Sons, 1958)
  The Prophetic Faith (New York, Harper Torchbooks, 1960)
  'The Heart Determines (Psalm 73)' in *On the Bible*
  (New York, Schoken Books, 1968)
  Tales of the Hasidim (New York, Schocken Books, 1991)

Cabaud, Jacques *'Simone Weil'* (London Harvill Press, 1964)

Camus, Albert, *The Stranger* (New York, Vintage Books, 1958)
  Caligula and Other Plays (New York, Vintage Books, 1958)
  The Plague (London, Penguin, 1960)
  The Fall (London, Penguin Classics, 2000)
  The Myth of Sisyphus (London, Penguin Classics, 2000)

Chavanes, Francois, *Albert Camus: Il Faut Vivre Maintenant* (Paris, Cerf, 1990)

Cox, D, *The Psalms in the Life of God's People*
  (Slough, St Paul's Publications, 1984)

Crenshaw, J, *A Whirlpool of Torment: Israelite Traditions of God as an Oppressive Presence* (OBT, Philadelphia, Fortress Press, 1984)

Crenshaw, James L, *Ecclesiastes* (OTL: Philadelphia, Westminster Press, 1987)

Cruickshank, John, *Albert Camus and the Literature of Revolt*
  (Oxford University Press, 1959)

Crusemann, Frank, 'The Unchangeable World: The Crisis of Wisdom in *Koheleth'* in *God of the Lowly*:
Sado-Historical Interpretations of the Bible (Eds. W Schottroff and W Stegemann, Maryknoll, Orbis Books, 1979)

Dahood, M, *Psalms* (3 vols: Anchor Bible 16, 17,17a)
  (Gordon City, New York, Doubleday, 1966, 1968, 1970)

Davidson, Robert, *The Vitality of Worship: A Commentary on the Book of Psalms* (Edinburgh, The Handel Press, 1998)
  The Courage to Doubt (London, SCM, 1983)

Dostoyevsky, Fyodor, *The Devils* (Harmondsworth: Penguin, 1953)
The Brothers Karamazov (Harmondsworth: Penguin, 1958)

Dylan, Bob, 'Tomorrow is a Long Time' from *Bob Dylan: Lyrics 1962-1985* (London, Paladin, 1987)

Einstein, Albert, *The World As I See It* (London, Bodley Head, 1955)

Fox, Michael V, *A Time to Tear Down and a Time to Build Up* (Cambridge, Eerdman, 1999)

Frankl, Viktor, *Man's Search for Meaning* (New York Pocket Books, 1985)
The Unconscious God (New York, Simon & Schuster, 1985)

Fretheim, Terence, *The Suffering of God* (OBT Philadelphia, Fortress Press, 1984)

Friedman, Maurice, *Martin Buber's Life and Work: The Early Years 1878-1923* (New York, EP Dutton, 1981) –
Martin Buber's Life and Work 1945-1965 (Detroit, Wayne State University Press, 1988)

Gaeta, Saverio, *Il Segreto di Madre Teresa* (Casile Monferrato, Piemme, 2003)

Gertsenberger, E S, *Psalms Part 1* (Grand Rapids, Eerdmans, 1988)
Psalms Part 2 and Lamentations (Grand Rapids, Eerdmans 2001)

Gordis, R, *The Book of God and Man: A Study of Job* (University of Chicago Press, 1969)
The Book of Job (New York, Jewish Theological Seminary of America, 1978)

Gunkel, H, *The Psalms: A Form - Critical Introduction* (Philadelphia, Fortress Press, 1967)

Guttirrez, Gustavo, *On Job* (New York, Orbis Books. 1999)

Habel, Norman C, *The Book of Job* (OTL, Philadelphia, Westminster Press, 1985)

Heschel, Abraham J, *Man's Quest for God*
(New York, Charles Schribner's Sons, 1954)
God in Search of Man: A Philosophy of Judaism
(New York, Farrar, Strauss and Cudahy, 1955)
'On Prayer: *Conservative Judaism, 25, No 1* (Fall, 1970) 1-14
The Prophets (New York, Jewish Publication Society of America, 1962)
Who is Man? (Stanford University Press, 1965)
The Insecurity of Freedom: Essays on Human Existence
(New York, Schocken Books, 1966)
'No Religion is an Island' in *No Religion is an Island*
(Eds. Harold Kasimow and Byron L Sherwin, Maryknoll, Orbis Books, 1991)
A Passion for Truth (Woodstock, Jewish Lights Publishing, 1995)

Hopkins, Gerard Manley, *The Works of Gerard Manley Hopkins*
(Ware, Hertfordshire, Wordsworth Editions, 1994)

Humphries, W Lee, *The Tragic Vision and the Old Testament*
(OBT, Philadelphia, Fortress Press, 1985)

Janzen, J Gerald, *Job: Interpretation* (Atlanta, John Knox Press, 1985)

Jinkins, M, *In the House of the Lord* (Collegeville, Liturgical Press, 1998)

Jung, C G, *Memories, Dreams, Reflections* (London, Fontana Press, 1995)

Sherwin, Byron, L (Ed.) *No Religion is an Island* (Maryknoll, Orbis Books, 1991)

Kafka, Franz, *The Trial* (London, Penguin, 1953)

Kazantzakis, Nikos, *Report to Greco* (Oxford, Cassier, 1965)

Kraus, H J, *Theology of the Psalms* (Minneapolis, Augsberg, 1986)

Kubler-Ross, Elizabeth, *On Death and Dying* (New York, Macmillan, 1969)

Larkin, Philip, *Collected Poems* (London, Marvell Press, 1988)

Marty, M, *A Cry of Absence* (New York, Harper and Row, 1983)

Mays, James L, *The Lord Reigns: A Theological Handbook to the Psalms*
(Louisville John Knox Press, 1994)
Psalms: Interpretation (Louisville, John Knox Press, 1994)

McCann, J Clinton, *A Theological Introduction to the Book of Psalms:*
The Psalms as Torah (Nashville, Abingdon Press, 1993)

McCarthy, John and Morrell, Jill, *Some Other Rainbow*
(London, Transworld, 1993)

McCuttchon, Stephen P, *Experiencing the Psalms*
(Macon, Ga Smyth, Helion, 2000)

Miller, P D, *Interpreting the Psalms* (Philadelphia, Fortress Press, 1986)
They Cried to the Lord: The Form and Theology of Biblical Prayer
(Minneapolis, Fortress Press, 1994)

Mitchell, Joni, 'The Sire of Sorrow (Job's Sad Song)' from the album
Turbulent Indigo (Regius Records, 1994)
'Slouching Towards Bethlehem' and 'God Must be a Boogie Man'
from the album *Travelogue* (Noneush Records, 2002)

Moltmann, Jurgen, *The Crucified God* (London, SCM Press, 1974)

Mowinckel, Sigmund, *The Psalms of Israel's Worship*
(Oxford, Oliver Blackwell, 1962)

Mumma, Howard, *Albert Camus and the Minister*
(Brewster, Mass., Paraclete Press, 2000)

Nouwen, Henri J M, *The Road to Daybreak*
(London, Danton, Longman and Todd, 1991)

Petremant, Simone, *Simone Weil: A Life* (New York, Pantheon Books,
1976)

Rouiller, Francis, *Le Scandale du Mal et de la Souffrance Chez Maurice Zundel*
(St-Maurice, Editions Saint- Augustin, 2002)

Soelle, D, *Suffering* (Philadelphia, Fortress Press, 1975)

Springsted, Eric O, *Simone Weil and the Suffering of Love*
(Cambridge, Cowley Publications, 1986)

Thérèse of Lisieux, *The Poetry of Saint Thérèse of Lisieux*
(Washington, ICS Publications, 2002)

Thompson, Francis, *Collected Poems* (Sevenoaks, Kent, Fisher Press, 1992)

Tillich, Paul, *The Courage to Be* (Yale University Press, 1952)
Systematic Theology - 3 vols (Chicago University Press, 1971)

Todd, Olivier, *Albert Camus: A Life* (New York, Carroll and Graf, 2000)

Van Breemen, Peter G, *As Bread That is Broken*
(New Jersey, Dimenssion Books, 1 974)

Von Balthasar, Hans Urs, *Tragedy Under Grace*
(San Francisco, Ignatius Press, 1988)

Waite, Terry, *Taken on Trust* (London, Hodder & Stoughton, 1993)

Weems, Ann, *Psalms of Lament*
(Louisville, Westminster John Knox Press, 1995)

Weil, Simone, *Waiting For God* (New York, Putman's Sons, 1951)
Intimations of Christianity Among the Ancient Greeks
(Boston, Beacon Pres, 1957)
Selected Writings, 'Modern Spiritual Masters' series
(New York, Orbis Books, 1998)

Weintraub, Simkay (Ed.), *Healing of Soul, Healing of Body*
(Woodstock, Jewish Lights Publishing, 1994)

Weiser, Arthur, *The Psalms* (OTL, Philadelphia, Westminister Press, 1962)

Westermann, Claus, *Praise and Lament in the Psalms*
(Atlanta, John Knox Press, 1981)
The Structure of the Book of Job (Philadelphia, Fortress Press, 1981)

Wiesel, Elie, *Night* (New York, Hill and Wang, 1960)

Wilde, Oscar, *Selected Poems,* Edited by Malcolm Hicks
(Manchester, Carcanet Press Ltd, 1992)

Wink W, *Engaging The Powers* (Minneapolis: Fortress Press, 1992)

Zundel, Maurice, *Hymne a la Joie* (Quebec, Editions A Sigier, 1992)
Quel Homme et Quel Dieu?
(Saint-Maurice, Editions Saint-Augustin, 1986)

Abbreviations

Old Testament

Genesis	Gn	Proverbs	Prv
Exodus	Ex	Qoheleth	Qo
Leviticus	Lv	Song of Songs	Sg
Numbers	Nm	Wisdom	Wis
Deuteronomy	Dt	Sirach	Sir
Joshua	Jos	Isaiah	Is
Judges	Jgs	Jeremiah	Jer
Ruth	Ru	Lamentations	Lam
1 Samuel	1 Sm	Baruch	Bar
2 Samuel	2 Sm	Ezekiel	Ez
1 Kings	I Kgs	Daniel	Dn
2 Kings	2 Kgs	Hosea	Hos
1 Chronicles	1 Chr	Joel	Jl
2 Chronicles	2 Chr	Amos	Am
Ezra	Ezr	Obadiah	Ob
Nehemiah	Neh	Jonah	Jon
Tobit	Tb	Micha	Mi
Judith	Jdt	Nahum	Na
Esther	Est	Habakkuk	Hb
1 Maccabees	1 Mc	Zephaniah	Zep
2 Maccabees	2 Mc	Haggai	Hg
Job	Job	Zechariah	Zee
Psalms	Ps(s)	Malachi	Mai

New Testament

Matthew	Mt	1 Corinthians	1 Cor
Mark	Mk	2 Corinthians	2 Cor
Luke	Lk	Galatians	
Gal			
John	Jn	Ephesians	
Eph			
Acts of the Apostles	Acts	Philippians	Phil
Romans	Rom	Colossians	Col

1 Thessalonians	1 Thes	1 Peter	1 Pt
2 Thessalonians	2 Thes	2 Peter	2 Pt
1 Timothy	1 Tim	I John	I Jn
2 Timothy	2 Tim	2 John	2 Jn
Titus	Ti	3 John	3Jn
Philemon	Phlm	Jude	Jude
Hebrews	Heb	Revelation	Rev
James	Jas		

Other Abbreviations

ABD	Anchor Bible Dictionary
BIB	Biblica
EH	Historia Ecclesiastica
CBQ	Catholic Biblical Quarterly
Int.	Interpretation
JR	Journal of Religion
NJBC	New Jerome Biblical Commentary
NTS	New Testament Studies
IQH	Thanksgiving Hymn for Quamran
RB	Revue Biblique
TDNT	Theological Word - Dictionary of the New Testament
ZNW	Zeitschrift fur die neu testamentliche Wissenschaft

Printed in Poland
by Amazon Fulfillment
Poland Sp. z o.o., Wrocław

63638751R00081